Contents

Cognitive enhancement

in Sport and Exercise Psychology

Edited by

Ian Cockerill

and

Hannah Steinberg

An occasional paper for the Sport and Exercise Psychology Section of The British Psychological Society, based on proceedings of a one-day workshop at the Institute of Education, London.

Published by The British Psychological Society, St Andrews House, 48 Princess Road East, Leicester LE1 7DR.

© 1997 The British Psychological Society

ISBN 1 85433 254 6

CONTRIBUTORS

Sarah Chamberlain
School of Sport and Exercise Sciences, University of Birmingham, B15 2TT

Dr Ian Cockerill
School of Sport and Exercise Sciences, University of Birmingham, B15 2TT

Alison Dewey
School of Psychology, Middlesex University, Enfield Campus, EN3 4SF

Richard Goodfellow
Department of Psychology, University of Central Lancashire, PR1 2HE

Dr Jan Graydon
West Sussex Institute of Higher Education, Chichester, PO19 4PE

Dr Tony Head
Department of Physical Education and Sport, Brunel University College, Osterley Campus, TW7 5DU

Marc Jones
Newman College of Higher Education, Birmingham, B32 3NT

Timothy Jones
41 Heyford Avenue, Bristol, BS5 4PE

Dr Roger Mace
Newman College of Higher Education, Birmingham, B32 3NT

Ken MacMahon
School of Sport and Exercise Sciences, University of Birmingham, B15 2TT

Dr Craig Mahoney
Department of Sports Studies, Roehampton Institute, London, SW15 3SN

Dr Richard Masters
School of Sport and Exercise Sciences, University of Birmingham, B15 2TT

Terry McMorris
West Sussex Institute of Higher Education, Chichester, PO19 4PE

Derek Milne
School of Neurosciences and Psychiatry, University of Newcastle, NE1 7RU

Jack Lamport-Mitchell
80 Grove Hill, South Woodford, E18 2HZ

Mark Nesti
School of Leisure and Sports Studies, Leeds Metropolitan University, LS6 3QS

Orla O'Leary

School of Leisure and Sports Studies, Leeds Metropolitan University, LS6 3QS

Dr David Sewell

Department of Psychology, University of Hull, HU6 7RX

David F. Shaw

Department of Psychology, University of Central Lancashire, PR1 2HE

Priscilla Simpson

School of Psychology, Middlesex University, Enfield Campus, EN3 4SF

Professor Hannah Steinberg

School of Psychology, Middlesex University, Enfield Campus, EN3 4SF

Claire Stockbridge

Newman College of Higher Education, Birmingham, B32 3NT

Professor Elizabeth A. Sykes

School of Psychology, Middlesex University, Enfield Campus, EN3 4SF

Preface

This is the fourth volume in a series of workshop proceedings published as BPS occasional publications by the Society's Sport and Exercise Psychology Section. Previous workshops were *Exercise Addiction: Motivation for Participation in Sport and Exercise; Quality and Quantity in Sport and Exercise Psychology* and *How Teams Work in Sport and Exercise Psychology*; copies are available from The British Psychological Society at £5 to members of the Section and £6 to non-members.

Normally the Section selects speakers by invitation and from an open announcement. On this occasion the response to the open announcement was considerable and it was decided that invitations were unnecessary. The topic of Cognitive Enhancement in Sport and Exercise was covered comprehensively, with most papers focusing upon the use of cognitive strategies for improving performance. Two papers took a different view by examining the role of exercise in improving cognitive skills, decision making and creative thinking.

There was a mix of tried and tested procedures standing alongside methods that were in the course of being developed by the speakers. Both qualitative and quantitative approaches to cognitive enhancement were highlighted, while laboratory-based studies of motor skills stood comfortably alongside those involving emotional control strategies for both groups and individuals.

The workshop was held on 18 December, 1996, during the Society's London Conference at the Institute of Education, University of London. There was a capacity audience with contributions from both postgraduates and established researchers. The Section thanks Dr Barry Cripps and Ann Cripps for their help throughout, and Valerie Bull and Geoff Ellis from the Society for their help and guidance in bring the publication to fruition, and Alison Dewey for her excellent co-ordinating work behind the scenes.

Ian M. Cockerill
Hannah Steinberg
June 1997

1

To think or not to think? That is the question! A discussion of the potential benefits of thinking less during sport

Tony Head

Timothy Gallwey, a philosopher and a psychologist, author of the popular *Inner Game* series of sports (psychology) books, has made a useful link between cognitive and behavioural strategies. He has written many books on the "inner skills" that are needed for tennis, golf and skiing. Gallwey suggests that such inner skills enable players to decrease the mental obstacles that prevent them from playing at their best. Two fundamental principles are involved in such a suggestion:

Principle 1: There are mental obstacles which prevent one from performing to one's best.

Principle 2: These obstacles can somehow be controlled or influenced.

Gallwey's approach of reducing mental obstacles contrasts with the traditional sports psychologist's approach of improving cognitive strategies to facilitate performance. He suggests that the inner skills of concentration, confidence and willpower can be improved by the reduction of mental obstacles, thereby improving the quality and consistency of performance. The focus of this paper is upon the skill of "concentration" (closed or fixed attention). Poor concentration can be defined as to draw the mind away in another direction, or to divert attention.

Posner and Boies (1971) have suggested that there are three aspects of *concentration:* alertness; the concept of a limited information processing capacity; and selective attention. Each of these will be discussed.

1) Alertness

The concept of alertness is closely related to arousal. Since Yerkes and Dodson (1908) and Hull (1943), arousal has been strongly linked with performance; the concept of an ideal or optimum state of arousal for each task/individual/situation is widely accepted within (sport) psychology (Martens and Landers, 1970; Oxendine, 1970; Fazey and Hardy, 1988). It is pertinent that the work of Yerkes and Dodson was behavioural in nature, focusing upon the "rapidity of habit formation". According to Skinner (1938), habit formation, more commonly described as learning, is the result of a purely mechanical connection between parts (i.e. stimulus, response and reward), and that inner mental events (cognition?) are no more necessary as an explanation of operant behaviour than they are of human physiological actions such as swallowing or the maintenance of posture (Skinner, 1938). According to Skinner, cognition in sport appears to be superfluous.

2) Limited information-processing capacity

This brings us to the second aspect of concentration described above, the idea of a limited human information-processing capacity, which explains the difficulty of performing two (novel) tasks at the same time. Once a task has been well learned, then little or no information-processing is necessary, leaving the limited information-processing capacity of the individual free to attend to other tasks. There is no contradiction between learning-theory and information processing as an explanation of behaviour. On the contrary, the two approaches complement one another. Thorndike (1905) and Skinner (1938) saw learned responses as subconscious and automated habits that require no information processing. Information processing incurs a time cost of approximately 150ms per bit of information processed. This is easily demonstrated with the increase in reaction time that occurs with multiple, rather than single, choices. Thus, responses that require less information to be processed are both fast and appropriate, providing that the best-learned response to a situation is the correct one (Hull and Spence, 1943), and that the performer is attending to the correct cues. Compared with the novice, experts are more likely to attend to the correct cues, thereby improving anticipation, even though they may not be aware of the cues or their strategy (Abernethy and Russell, 1987). If performers are unaware of the cues or their strategy, it suggests that such responses operate at a sub-conscious level (Gallwey's Self 2) as suggested by Thorndike (1905) and Skinner (1938).

3) Selective attention

The third aspect of concentration described by Posner and Boies (1971) is selective attention. The work of Cherry (1953) described how an individual at a cocktail party can listen to a conversation whilst ignoring other conversations in the same room. Cherry (1953) investigated the ability of individuals to attend to simultaneously-presented data and concluded that we are severely limited in our abilities to recall information that is presented whilst attending to other information. However, when an individual's name is mentioned, then his/her attention is gained. This concept is used in aviation radiotelephony, where the call sign of the aircraft (well known to the pilot) precedes any message that follows. This ensures that the pilot's attention is directed toward the ensuing message, whilst messages intended for other aircraft are ignored. The novice student pilot has difficulty with the multi-tasks of controlling the aircraft, talking to controllers and noting and subsequently reacting to information given. With training, however, the action of flying control becomes automated, requiring little information processing, and is nothing more than a sequence of learned, automated (conditioned) responses to visual and auditory stimuli. Just as the pilot – consciously at first and then subconsciously when the skill is well-conditioned – directs attention to primary flight instruments, the sports performer can also learn to selectively attend to specific cues that improve performance. For example, to improve the return of passing shots in tennis, the appropriate cues would appear to be the racket and forearm of the opposing player (Buckholz et al., 1988), and it is attention to these cues that will improve performance in predicting the type of shot to be played.

Therefore, with situations that require either very simple automated responses, and also those that appear to demand complex actions such as piloting an aeroplane, "cognitive" strategies would appear to be largely superfluous. However, lapses in concentration may still cause losses in performance through missed cues or attention to incorrect cues. Gallwey (1981) offered strategies that may improve – or at least maintain – performance by optimizing concentration and directing the attention of the subconscious (Self 2) to relevant cues.

He argued that there are two "selves". Self 1 is most closely related to the conscious thinking mind, and Self 2 most closely related to the sub-conscious mind. Gallwey believed that whilst Self 2 wants to, and is capable of, performing complex motor skills reliably, Self 1 interferes with and inhibits Self 2's natural responses to situations. Running downstairs is a good example of this concept; most of us are capable of running downstairs quite quickly if necessary and we do not have to think about foot placement because the skill is well conditioned. However, if one actively thinks about foot placement, then errors occur.

Performance: Self 1 and Self 2

Errors that occur when a player has time to think about a stroke in, say, tennis or squash are, according to Gallwey, produced by a lapse of concentration. A common expression in games is that the player has "too much time to think", and that indecision forces errors. Gallwey offered strategies which occupy the conscious mind (Self 1) so that it does not interfere with skill execution (by Self 2). The crucial and exquisite point of the strategies that Gallwey proposed is that they always involve a cue that is relevant to the execution of a skill. In the simplest form of "The Inner Game", a tennis player might be instructed to say "bounce" precisely as the ball bounces in front of him, and "hit" as his racket makes contact with the ball. Initially, the player says such words overtly and progresses to covert verbalization once correct timing has been achieved. Thus the player is forced to attend to the trajectory, pace and spin of the ball, together with the timing and trajectory of the racket, all of which are crucial cues and need attending to if stroke execution is to be successful. If the player says "bounce" or "hit" out of phase (i.e. too early or too late), then it is assumed that he/she must be "thinking" (i.e. Self 1 is processing information) about how to execute the shot, which should not be necessary if the response is already well-conditioned. If the player concentrates on co-ordinating the verbalization of the sound with bounce and contact, then Gallwey argued that Self 1 is too occupied by the task to interfere with the execution of the skill. This concept fits well with the concept of a limited information-processing channel described by Posner and Boies (1971). The idea that Self 2 operates automatically (i.e. without conscious processing) to cues or stimuli, also fits nicely with Skinnerian (1938) concepts of behaviourism without excluding cognition (by Self 1). Thus, Gallwey may have produced a solution to a century's worth of conflict between cognitive and behavioural psychologists. Much practical research is now required to put Gallwey's concepts to the test in carefully-controlled situations. Perhaps sport psychology should focus on behaviourism as much as cognition. Gallwey offered similarly intuitive insights into improvement of confidence and willpower and, whilst his explanations are usually anecdotally-based, they are in conflict with the mainstream strategies of imagery (Block 1981), self-talk (Rushall et al., 1988) and self-efficacy (Bandura, 1977), and deserve attention from researchers. In the future we may even consider "How to stop thinking altogether to improve performance".

References

Abernethy, B. and Russell, D.G. (1987) Expert-Novice Differences in an applied selective attention task. *Journal of Sport Psychology, 9*, pp. 326–345.

Buckholz, E., Prapavesis, H. and Fairs, J. (1988) Advance cues and their use in predicting tennis passing shots. *Canadian Journal of Sport Science, 13,* pp. 20–30.

Bandura, A. (1977) Self-efficacy: toward a unifying theory of behavioural change. *Psychological Review, 84,* 191–215.

Block, N. (Ed.) (1981) *Imagery.* Cambridge, MA: MIT Press.

Cherry, E.C. (1953) Some experiments on the recognition of speech, with one and two ears. *Journal of the Acoustical Society of America, 25,* pp. 975–979.

Fazey, J. and Hardy, L. (1988) The inverted-U hypothesis: a catastrophe for sport psychology? *British Association of Sports Sciences Monograph, no.1.* Leeds: The National Coaching Foundation.

Gallwey, W.T. (1981) *The Inner Game of Golf.* Jonathan Cape Ltd.

Hull, C.L. (1943) *Principles of Behavior.* New York: Appleton-Century-Crofts, pp. 14–16.

Martens, R. and Landers, D.M. (1970) Motor performance under stress: a test of the inverted-U hypothesis. *Journal of Personality and Social Research, 16,* pp. 29–37.

Oxendine, J.B. (1970) Emotional arousal and motor performance. *Quest, 13,* pp. 23–30.

Posner, M.I. and Boies, S.J. (1971) Components of Attention. *Psychological Review, 78,* pp. 391–408.

Skinner, B.F. (1938) *The Behavior of Organisms.* New York: Appleton-Century-Croft, p.13.

Rushall, B.S., Hall, M. and Rushall, A. (1988) Effects of three types of thought content instructions on skiing performance. *The Sport Psychologist, 2,* pp. 283–297.

Thorndike, E.L. (1907) *The Elements of Psychology.* 2nd edition. New York: A.G. Seiler (first published 1905), p12.

Yerkes, R.M. and Dodson, J.D. (1908) The relationship of strength of stimulus to rapidity of habit formation. *Journal of Comparative Neurology and Psychology, 18,* pp. 459–482.

2

The effect of incremental exercise on decision-making in soccer-specific tests

Terry McMorris and Jan Graydon

Many researchers have examined the effect of exercise on the performance of laboratory-based cognitive tasks, such as simple reaction time (McMorris and Keen, 1994), choice reaction time (Chmura et al., 1994), coincident anticipation (Isaacs and Pohlman, 1991) and short-term memory (Davey, 1973). These authors have generally hypothesized that exercise of a moderate intensity improves performance, while heavy exercise results in a deterioration back to base level. In other words, an inverted-U effect will be demonstrated.

Tomporowski and Ellis (1986) claimed that because exercise is a stressor it affects cognitive functioning in the same way as emotionally-induced somatic arousal. They drew upon Easterbrook's (1959) cue utilization theory to support their contention that exercise has an inverted-U effect on cognitive performance. According to Easterbrook, at low levels of arousal the individual attends to few cues, relevant or irrelevant. At moderate levels of arousal the individual's attention is optimal and they will attend only to task-relevant information. As arousal increases further, attention narrows until even task-relevant cues are missed. However, inspection of research results provides little support for this claim (see McMorris and Keen, 1994, for a summary).

Tomporowski and Ellis (1986) claimed that the failure to support unequivocally an inverted-U hypothesis was due to poor control over the exercise protocols, in particular the failure to take into account individual differences in fitness levels. McMorris and Keen (1994), however, showed that in experiments in which individual differences had been accounted for, the evidence was still far from conclusive. Tomporowski and Ellis also claimed that differences in the complexity of the laboratory-based tasks may have affected the results. However, their data tend to show that there are equivocal findings for both simple and complex tasks.

McMorris and Graydon (in press, a) argue that the problem was not the complexity of the laboratory tasks, but their unfamiliarity. They claim that habituation and learning may have contaminated the result and decided to test this hypothesis with experienced soccer players on a soccer-specific test of decision making. Participants were tested with three versions of a soccer decision-making test: at rest and while exercising at 70 per cent and 100 per cent of their maximum power output (MPO). The experimental task consisted of slides of typical game situations which were presented to the participants on a slide projector fitted with a tachistoscope. The tachistoscope initiated a voice-reaction timer when the slide was illuminated. Participants had to state as quickly and as accurately as possible what action the player in possession of the ball should take. There were four options: run, shoot, pass or dribble. Speed and accuracy of decision were the dependent variables.

The results, however, did not demonstrate an inverted-U effect. A Repeated Measures Multivariate Analysis of Variance (RM MANOVA) and *post-hoc* Tukey tests showed that there was a linear improvement in performance as exercise intensity increased. It was argued that these results were due to the task being familiar to the subjects; thus high levels of arousal would produce optimal performance, as found by Oxendine (1984). To test this claim, McMorris and Graydon (1996a) repeated their experiment, but this time they tested both experienced and inexperienced players.

A significant experience exercise-intensity interaction effect supported the contention that familiarity with the task would result in differences for players and non-players. The direction of the results was not, however, as McMorris and Graydon (1996a) had hypothesized. Experienced players demonstrated similar results to those in the first experiment (McMorris and Graydon, in press, a), except that there was no significant difference between performance at 70 per cent and 100 per cent MPO. Inexperienced players produced no significant effect of exercise on performance. The results, however, were not straightforward. While the omnibus statistics, a Doubly Multivariate Multiple Analysis Of Variance (DM MANOVA), demonstrated a significant effect of exercise on decision making, a separate univariate Repeated Measures Analyses of Variance (RM ANOVAs) showed that only speed of response had contributed significantly to the results. Accuracy did not differ significantly across exercise intensities for either set of participants. Similar effect had been observed in the first experiment (McMorris and Graydon, in press, a); this was not surprising for experienced players. One would have expected the inexperienced players to be negatively affected during maximal exercise. McMorris and Graydon (1996a) claimed that the test may have lacked complexity, even for the inexperienced participants, for an inverted-U effect to be demonstrated. Consequently, they decided to compare soccer players' performance on the original test and on a more complex test (McMorris and Graydon, 1996b).

An RM MANOVA showed that the complex test was indeed significantly more difficult than the simple test, and separate univariate RM ANOVAs showed that both speed and accuracy contributed significantly to the results. The expected test by exercise-intensity interaction effect was not demonstrated. There was a significant main effect for exercise intensity and, once again, the separate univariate RM ANOVAs showed that accuracy did not contribute significantly to the results. There were significant increases in speed of decision as exercise intensity rose. McMorris and Graydon (1996b) felt that the speed-accuracy trade off may have affected accuracy. They thought it possible that subjects were concentrating on speed in all conditions, hence the failure of accuracy to be affected by exercise. Therefore, they tested two separate groups of experienced soccer players on the complex decision-making test. One group was instructed to answer as quickly and accurately as possible, while the other group was told that time was not being examined and to concentrate on accuracy. In fact, both speed of response and accuracy were the dependent variables. A DM MANOVA showed significant main effects for instructional set and exercise-intensity, but a non-significant instructional set by exercise intensity interaction effect. Speed of decision at rest was significantly slower than during exercise at 100 per cent MPO. There were no other significant differences.

McMorris and Graydon (in press, b) considered that the nature of the tachistoscopically presented decision-making task may have been the reason for the results. The first task for the subject in such tests is to search for the ball position. This is a simple visual-search task and, according to Oxendine (1984), the task should be facilitated by high levels of arousal. Thus, it was decided to test the hypothesis by examining the effect of exercise on speed of ball detection. It was further argued that familiarity with the display may affect the results; therefore speed of search in game and non-game displays were examined.

The results showed a main effect for exercise but no display-by-exercise interaction effect. Speed of ball detection at 100 per cent MPO was significantly faster than in the other two conditions, which did not differ significantly from one another. Although this supports the hypothesis, the decrease in mean times from rest to maximal exercise showed that the difference was not as great as those found in the previous experiments. Thus, the authors argued that perhaps an increase in speed of visual search was not the only cause of the results in previous experiments.

In order to determine whether speed of ball detection was the only factor affecting increases in speed of decision making, or if the whole decision-making process was affected, McMorris and Graydon (in press, b) carried out a further experiment. Participants were tested on the simple decision-making test, but situations were added in which no ball was present. The tachistoscope activated not only the voice reaction timer but also a finger reaction timer. In those slides in which a ball was present, participants had to press the button when they saw the ball; this represented the speed of the visual search dependent variable. Once the ball had been spotted, the participant had to say what action the player in possession should take. This was the total decision time dependent variable. The difference in time from spotting the ball to making the decision was calculated and acted as a third dependent variable. Accuracy was the fourth dependent variable.

An RM MANOVA demonstrated a significant effect of exercise. The separate RM ANOVAs showed that speed of ball detection did not contribute significantly to the results. The other variables did contribute. Tukey post-hoc tests showed that for total decision time, speed at rest was significantly different from the other two conditions, which did not differ significantly from one another. For speed of decision following ball detection, speed during maximal exercise was significantly faster than in the other two conditions. The authors claimed that these results showed that it was most likely that the speed of the entire decision-making process was increased by exercise. They contended that the different results from the previous experiment for speed of ball detection was probably due to participants using different preparatory sets for the two experiments. They asserted that in this experiment participants did not merely search for the presence or absence of the ball, but processed the relevant information required to make a decision while searching for the ball.

Summary and conclusion

Exercise at 100 per cent MPO was shown unequivocally to induce and increase speed of decision-making among subjects for whom the task was familiar. Performance during exercise at 70 per cent MPO produced equivocal results, although the general trend was to demonstrate a linear increase in decision speed. In all but one experiment, accuracy was unaffected by exercise intensity. In the one experiment where it was affected (McMorris and Graydon, in press, b), the effect size and difference in group means were small. Moreover, the results were in the opposite direction to that predicted by arousal theories, with maximal exercise producing an improvement in performance.

The results do not support the contention of Tomporowski and Ellis (1986) that exercise will affect cognitive performance in an inverted-U manner, neither do they support the claims of Oxendine (1984) that simple and complex tasks will be affected differently. The results for speed of decision provide some support for allocatable resources theories (Kahneman, 1973; Humphreys and Revelle, 1984; Eysenck,1992). According to these theories, as arousal level increases so does the amount of allocatable resources available to the central nervous system (CNS). This could be due to exercise inducing increases in the neurotransmitters adrenaline and noradrenaline (Chmura et al., 1994). Logically, information would be able to be processed more quickly if more resources were available. According to these theories, however, the key factor is the allocation of resources, which is the role of what is termed cognitive effort. Kahneman, and Humphreys and Revell (1984), however, claimed that at high levels of arousal the CNS is unable to allocate resources solely to task-specific purposes and therefore performance will deteriorate. Eysenck (1992) argued that this is not necessarily the case and that it may be possible for highly-motivated people to allocate resources appropriately.

However, McMorris and Keen's (1994) claim that even maximal exercise may not equate with high levels of arousal should be considered. As they point out, when individuals are exercising, even maximally, they are in a state of homeostasis. Highly emotionally aroused individuals are not in a state of homeostasis, therefore one cannot equate maximal exercise with maximal arousal. It is possible that exercise at 100 per cent MPO represents a moderate level of arousal for fit subjects who are used to performing at this intensity. It is unlikely that they would allocate resources to non-task relevant information, such as feelings of discomfort and pain.

These arguments do not explain the somewhat equivocal results for exercise during 70 per cent MPO. Davis (1985) and Chmura et al. (1994) have shown that the rate of changes in plasma levels of adrenaline and noradrenaline from rest to those during moderate intensity of exercise vary greatly between individuals. Thus, the equivocal results may be attributed to individual differences. At maximal exercise it would appear safe to assume that all subjects have reached high levels of adrenaline and noradrenaline.

The results for accuracy of decision can also be accounted for by the notion of allocation of resources. If individuals can, by cognitive effort, attend to task relevant-cues even when in a low arousal state (Eysenck,1992; Humphreys and Revelle, 1984; Kahneman, 1973) and even when arousal level is high (Eysenck), then there appears to be no reason why accuracy of decision should change. Accuracy would presumably only change if attention was disrupted by resources being allocated to non-task-relevant information.

References

Chmura, J., Nazar, K. and Kaciuba-Uscilko, H. (1994). Choice reaction time during graded exercise in relation to blood lactate and plasma catecholamines thresholds. *International Journal of Sports Medicine, 15,* 172–176.

Davis, J. A. (1985). Anaerobic threshold: review of the concept and direction for future research. *Medicine and Science in Sports and Exercise, 17,* 6–18.

Davey, C. P. (1973). Physical exertion and mental performance. *Ergonomics, 16,* 595–599.

Easterbrook, J. A. (1959). The effect of emotion on cue utilization and the organization of behavior. *Psychological Review, 66,* 183–201.

Eysenck, M. (1992). *Anxiety: The Cognitive Perspective.* Hove: Lawrence Erlbaum Associates.

Humphreys, M. S. and Revelle, W. (1984). Personality, motivation, and performance: a theory of the relationship between individual differences and information processing. *Psychological Review, 91,* 153–184.

Isaacs, L. D. and Pohlman, E. L. (1991). Effects of exercise intensity on an accompanying timing task. *Journal of Human Movement Studies, 20,* 123-131.

Kahneman, D. (1973). *Attention and Effort.* Englewood Cliffs, NJ: Prentice Hall.

McMorris, T. and Graydon, J. (1996a). Effect of exercise on the decision-making performance of experienced and inexperienced soccer players. *Research Quarterly for Exercise and Sport, 67,* 109–114.

McMorris, T. and Graydon, J. (1996b). Effect of exercise on soccer decision-making tasks of differing complexities. *Journal of Human Movement Studies, 320,* 177–193.

McMorris, T. and Graydon, J. (in press, a) Effect of exercise on the decision-making performance of college soccer players.

McMorris, T. and Graydon, J. (in press, b) The effect of exercise on cognitive performance in soccer specific tests.

McMorris, T. and Keen, P. (1994). Effect of exercise on simple reaction time of recreational athletes. *Perceptual and Motor Skills, 78,* 123–130.

Oxendine, J. B. (1984). *Psychology of Motor Learning.* Englewood Cliffs, NJ: Prentice Hall.

Tomporowski, P. D. and Ellis, N. R. (1986). Effect of exercise on cognitive processes: a review. *Psychological Bulletin, 99,* 338–346.

3

Anxiety control and performance in figure skating

Mark Nesti and Dave Sewell

Stress management and anxiety control have received considerable attention within the sport and exercise psychology literature in recent years. Studies investigating the efficacy of various interventions on stress management and anxiety control in sport (e.g. Elko and Ostrow, 1991) have frequently employed sport-specific trait anxiety and state anxiety inventories. In addition, the Competitive State Anxiety Inventory - 2 (CSAI - 2; Martens et al., 1990) increasingly has been used to determine athletes' cognitive anxiety and somatic anxiety levels and self-confidence rating. Jones (1990) reported that relaxation strategies have typically been used in anxiety control studies in sport. Further development of this has involved evaluating the effectiveness of using somatic intervention techniques to manage somatic anxiety, and using cognitively-based techniques to reduce cognitive anxiety, following Davidson and Schwartz's (1976) *matching hypothesis*. In their study of semi-professional footballers, Maynard et al. (1995) provided some support for the matching hypothesis, at least for somatic anxiety symptoms.

A common feature of most studies of stress, anxiety and performance in sport has been that competitive anxiety has been viewed almost universally as a problem and something to be avoided or controlled. In response to this rather one-sided interpretation of anxiety, Jones et al. (1994) utilized CSAI -2 with an additional scale to measure facilitative and debilitative dimensions of anxiety in elite and non-elite athletes. They found that the elite swimmers in the study viewed anxiety as more facilitative of performance than did non-elite swimmers. Despite this finding, self-help sport psychology texts, research articles and coach education resources (e.g. National Coaching Foundation Mental Skills Training Programme – Anxiety Control, 1990) convey a clear message that anxiety presents a problem, rather than a challenge or an aid to enjoyment and improved performance.

Conceptualizing anxiety and the use of interventions

Given the prominence accorded to anxiety (rather than stress) in existential psychology (e.g. May, 1977), it seems remarkable that this body of literature has been given so little consideration in the study of anxiety in sport. This is all the more surprising in the light of the emphasis that this approach places on the potential for anxiety to be used productively, and on distinctions between normal anxiety and neurotic anxiety (May, 1977). According to this "school" of psychology, normal anxiety is not a problem and is generally linked to growth, whilst neurotic anxiety develops from un-met normal anxiety and may result in "closing off" and withdrawal from challenging situations. Such an interpretation of anxiety in competitive sport could begin to improve understanding about why some athletes seem to view high anxiety levels favourably. Calls for more radical approaches to the topic by Martens (1987), and exhortation by Jones and Hardy (1990) for more use of single-subject multiple-baseline designs, has had little obvious effect to date.

The use of trait approaches has dominated sports-anxiety research since its earliest days. It is suggested that this situation has largely arisen because of the ease with which psychometric measures can be used to rate anxiety levels. In addition, these apparently rigorous and objective instruments provide valid and reliable data upon which anxiety control intervention programmes can be based. However, given the paucity of research aimed at conceptualizing the exact nature of anxiety in sport, and the oft-mentioned confusion over the terms stress, anxiety and arousal in the sports literature (Jones and Hardy, 1990), questions remain.

In general, intervention programmes such as Anxiety Management Training (Suinn and Richardson, 1971) and Stress Inoculation Training (Meichenbaum, 1985) have been used in several studies investigating the effects of stress and anxiety on performance. Within sport, Mace (1990) suggests that many intervention studies have failed to consider either placebo effects or the use of longitudinal designs. A further weakness of the extant literature on anxiety and intervention strategies is that few studies have considered youth sport, while researchers have only recently begun to consider individual experiences and interpretations of stress (e.g. Gould, Jackson and Finch, 1993).

A range of self-help manuals, audio tapes and educational resources aimed at stress management and anxiety control in sport are available to coaches and athletes at all levels of performance. Within the UK, the NCF, in its capacity as the official coach education arm of the Sports Council, has developed a series of modules to help athletes to enhance their mental skills. Booklets and accompanying tapes are available on anxiety control, mental rehearsal, goal setting and concentration training. Within each, different strategies and techniques are explained and exercises are provided to assist learning.

The efficacy of anxiety-control interventions in youth sport

At Leeds Metropolitan University and the University of Hull we have focused upon age-group swimmers, rugby league players, and young ice skaters. An investigation into the use of anxiety control strategies and performance in skating has been undertaken with 15 female skaters. Their ages ranged from 11 to 17 years (mean = 14 years 2 months); competitive skating experience ranged from 16 months to 5 years (mean = 3 years 11 months). The CSAI -2 was administered to the skaters one hour before a competition, and in-depth interviews focusing on anxiety and performance were completed on a separate occasion. Further data emerged from coach (N=5) and judge (N=2) ratings on skaters' somatic anxiety and cognitive anxiety levels at a simulated competitive event. Performances were videotaped at this event and viewed and scored independently by coaches to ensure inter-observer reliability. Finally, the skaters themselves responded to a short questionnaire to describe how they felt during the event and to report experiences of anxiety. Transcripts of the athlete interviews were analysed using a phenomenological method, referred to as phenomenography by Marton (1981). This involves looking at certain aspects of the data, for example those relating to competitive anxiety, rather than allowing patterns to emerge spontaneously. Thus, the data are interpreted within a preconceived conceptual overlay.

Skaters were subsequently assigned to one of three groups (n=5): a control group of randomly selected skaters, a group of skaters experiencing the highest level of somatic anxiety, and a group of skaters experiencing the highest levels of cognitive anxiety. The skaters were taught relaxation and anxiety-control strategies appropriate to their needs, based on the NCF anxiety control mental-training programme. They were instructed in the skills and strategies by an accredited sport psychologist for a total of eight 45-minute sessions during which the relevant coach was in attendance. Finally, skaters were encouraged to incorporate these skills within their pre-performance routines and to practice them at training each day.

The principal finding of the study was that anxiety levels had not altered after an eight-week individually-tailored anxiety-control intervention programme. Re-assessment of cognitive anxiety levels and somatic anxiety levels through in-depth semi-structured interviews of skaters and coaches, and completion of CSAI - 2, failed to provide support for the matching hypothesis. The mean anxiety scores reported in Table 1 support the results of the more qualitatively focused parts of the study. Interestingly, a closer inspection of these data revealed that four out of five skaters in the control group felt more self-confident and motivated and that, according to the coaches, there had been improvements in performance and anxiety control.

	Highest Cognitive Group (n=5)		Highest Somatic Group (n=5)		Control (n=5)	
	Cognitive Mean Sd	Somatic Mean Sd	Cognitive Mean Sd	Somatic Mean Sd	Cognitive Mean Sd	Somatic Mean Sd
Pre-intervention	22.3 4.2	14.1 2.8	17.9 5.3	16.2 7.3	16.2 5.4	12.7 5.1
Post-intervention	23.6 6.1	15.0 4.1	15.9 4.6	16.9 5.4	13.6 6.1	11.3 4.2

Table 1. Mean anxiety scores for the three groups as measured by CSAI - 2

Conclusions

In contrast to work by Maynard et al. (1995), no support was found for the matching hypothesis. Analysis of post-intervention interviews revealed that the young female ice skaters were not motivated to learn the relevant anxiety control techniques and that they felt that the programme, although objectively tailored on the basis of assessment, had largely failed to meet their subjective needs.

An important theme that emerged was that mental skills are perhaps learned best by young athletes as an integral part of their sport experience and that where possible this work should be the responsibility of the coach. Although the coaches involved provided full and active support throughout all stages of the programme, feedback confirmed that they were surprised at the naiveté of an accredited sport psychologist in expecting anything more from the skaters than mere behavioural adherence to the programme. Of crucial importance to this study, compared with most others (e.g. Maynard et al., 1995), was that subjects were largely high-level female teenage athletes involved in a very physically and emotionally demanding sport where, according to Gould et al. (1993), there are considerable expectations and pressures to perform well and a strong emphasis on maintaining low body-weight and an attractive physical appearance. This contextual factor may help to explain why several skaters in the control group appeared to benefit from their involvement in the study. In order to meet ethical requirements, skaters in the control group were involved in one-to-one discussions of a general nature with an accredited sport psychologist for 15 minutes each week. Discussions were led by the athlete and tended to focus on skating generally; no attempt was made to direct the skater's attention to anxiety, motivation or other specific areas. It may be argued that the study demonstrates that objective assessment techniques and distance-learning packages can provide a useful framework for some athletes. However, it may be that for youth athletes in particular, if longer-term intervention aimed at anxiety control is to be effective it must involve counselling.

In addition, the findings of this study question the validity of vigorously promoting the use of self-help audio tapes and booklets with youth athletes, and suggest that anxiety-control strategies should be taught by coaches throughout an individual's sport life, and where anxiety is severe and debilitating it should be addressed by qualified psychologists or counsellors. In terms of generating new methods for investigating the anxiety and performance relationship in sport, research at the University of Hull represents an attempt to combine qualitative and quantitative approaches to improve conceptual vigour and predictive power. Recent work (e.g. Clough et al., 1996) on the use of diaries in sport and exercise settings provides a promising step forward in this area of work, going some way towards finding a methodology that yields data both rich in meaning and amenable to measurement. This could assist researchers in identifying baseline anxiety levels for individuals and help to contextualize sports participation, anxiety, self-confidence and motivation levels within a broader framework encompassing other important aspects of an athlete's daily life, such as family and work commitments.

Acknowledgements
We particularly wish to thank coaches Donna Gately, Debbie Watson, and Karen White for their patient and helpful support with this study.

References

Clough, P., Hockey, R. and Sewell, D. (1996) The use of a diary methodology to assess the impact exercise on mental states. In C. Robson, B. Cripps and H. Steinberg (Eds) *Qualitative and Quantitative Research Methods in Sport and Exercise Psychology*, pp. 22–27. Leicester: British Psychological Society.

Davidson, R.J. and Schwartz, G.E. (1976) The psychobiology of relaxation and related states: A multiprocess theory. In D.I. Mostofsky (Ed.) *Behavioural Control and Modification of Physiological Activity*, pp. 399–442. Englewood Cliffs, NJ: Prentice Hall.

Elko, K.P. and Ostrow. A.C. (1991) Effects of a rational-emotive education program on heightened anxiety levels of female collegiate gymnastics. *The Sport Psychologist, 5*, 235–255.

Gould, D., Jackson, S.A. and Finch, L. (1993) Life at the top: The experiences of US national champion figure skaters. *The Sports Psychologist, 7*, 354–374.

Jones, J.G. and Hardy, L. (1990) *Stress and Performance in Sport*. Chichester: Wiley.

Jones, J.G. (1990) Multi-dimensional anxiety and performance. In J.G. Jones and L. Hardy (Eds), *Stress and Performance in Sport*, pp. 43–80. Chichester: Wiley.

Jones, J.G., Hanton, S. and Swain, A (1994) Intensity and interpretation of anxiety symptoms in elite and non-elite sports performers. *Journal of Personality and Individual Differences, 17*, 657–663.

Mace, R. (1990). Cognitive behavioural interventions in sport. In J.G. Jones and L. Hardy (Eds), *Stress and Performance in Sport*, pp. 203–230. Chichester: Wiley

Martens, R., Burton, D., Vealey, R.S., Bump, L.A. and Smith, D.E. (1990) The Competitive State Anxiety Inventory -2. In R. Martens, R. Vealey and D. Burton (Eds). *Competitive Anxiety in Sport*. Champaign Il: Human Kinetics.

Martens, R. (1987) Science, knowledge and sport psychology. *The Sport Psychologist, 1*, 29–55.

Marton, F. (1981) Phenomenography: describing conceptions of the world around us. *Instructional Science, 10*, 177–200.

May, R. (1977) *The Meaning of Anxiety*. New York : Ronald Press.

Maynard, I.W., Hemmings, B., and Warwick-Evans, L. (1995) The effects of a somatic intervention strategy on competitive state anxiety and performance in semi-professional soccer players. *The Sport Psychologist, 9*, 51–64.

Meichenbaum, D. (1985) *Stress Inoculation Training*. New York: Pergamon.

Mental Training Programme (1990) *Anxiety Control – A guide for Sports Performers*. Leeds: The National Coaching Foundation.

Suinn, R.E. and Richardson, F. (1971) Anxiety management training: a non-specific behaviour therapy program for anxiety control, *Behaviour Therapy, 2*, 498–510.

The stimulation of memory for success, by the Achievement Bank Book

Jack Lamport-Mitchell

Many consultations between athletes and sport psychologists involve the client in providing an inordinate amount of negative information. It appears that sportsmen and sportswomen are not only upset by mistakes and failure, they seem to spend many hours rehearsing these experiences through negative self-talk. It is no wonder that this information is well ingrained in memory.

This paper will illustrate this phenomenon with some cases histories using a technique I devised called "The Achievement Bank Book"(ABB), a method to help clients both to stimulate the memory for positive experiences and achievements and also to provide a "Bank Book" of these achievements for later rehearsal. Perna (1995) described a cognitive-behavioural programme which was carried out with Li Wa – a gymnast who was injured falling from a vaulting horse. A few months later she was able to return to full-time training, but her confidence had left her and she was referred to a sport psychologist. Perna described how the sessions were dominated by negative self-talk concerning her ability and athletic future.

Many athletes use absolute statements to describe their performance or ability. For example "I can't hit a ball straight"; "I can't play golf"; "I am not a professional footballer". Ellis (1995) identified this phenomenon in his psychotherapeutic work and his method of dealing with it was called Rational Emotive Therapy (RET).

In my own practice, a figure skater who had recently fallen while trying to execute a triple jump told me that she would never complete one again. I saw a professional footballer who had been injured for some time, who was physically cured and had spent many months undergoing physiotherapy. When I asked him what he did for a living he told me that he "wasn't a professional footballer". I refuted this statement by telling him I had seen him play professional football on television and had read about him in newspapers. A professional golfer spent two hours in one session telling me how his "golfing game had gone" and various other negative factors about his performances on a number of golf courses. It later transpired that two years previously he had undertaken a very successful tour of Australia but he had told me nothing of this positive experience. I ran a session with a squad of rugby union players and asked each of them to tell me about certain games where they played really well. None of the players answered my question but told me instead how poorly they had performed. It was only in consultation with other players that some of these athletes agreed they had performed very well recently.

From my experience of persistence in negative self-talk by athletes, I tried to devise a technique to stimulate the athletes to recall positive information about his or her experiences. This technique I called "Achievement Bank Book". The idea came to me in 1986 when I worked as an occupational psychologist on an out-placement programme for company employees facing redundancy. Each member of the Group was asked to spend time recalling and writing down their achievements and positive aspects of their personality. I started to use this method with my clients in the following way.

Phase 1. I would see a new client and build a trusting relationship with them.
Phase 2. I would ask the client to relate to me their athletic history, where the emphasis of many was negative.
Phase 3. We discussed ways of working towards future success using a number of techniques and homework tasks including the Achievement Bank Book. In their own time, clients were encouraged to brainstorm any successes and achievements in their life from a very early age to the present. This can be done initially on rough paper. The client then transposes this information in chronological order into a notebook, finally recording information about their athletic performances. The process of writing down this information seems to have a therapeutic effect. Clients have returned saying that they had forgotten the many achievements in their life, let alone in their sport. The actual exercise of recording the information twice seemed to have the effect of making it indelible on their minds.

The client was then asked to write their own name and date on the front cover of the book and call it their Achievement Bank Book. At those times when they lacked confidence, they could always dip into the book to remind themselves of their successes. The Achievement Bank Book is never in the red!

References

Perna, P., Meyer, M., Murphy, S.M. (1995) *Sport Psychology Interventions.* USA: Human Kinetics Publications

Ellis, A. (1975) *Humanistic Psychotherapy: An RET approach.* McGraw Hill: New York.

Implicit motor learning: Suppression as a solution

Ken MacMahon, Richard Masters and Sarah Chamberlain

Masters (1992), replicated by Hardy et al. (1996), demonstrated that motor skills learnt implicitly (i.e. with little explicit verbal knowledge about the skill) are more resistant to breakdown under stress than those skills learnt in a more traditional, explicit manner.

In these studies, a concurrent secondary task (random-letter-generation – Baddeley, 1966) was used to bring about implicit learning. Despite success in preventing the accumulation of explicit knowledge, the difficulty of the random-letter-generation task led to significantly poorer performance during learning, when the implicit groups were compared with explicit groups not required to perform the secondary task. Thus, in order for findings about resistance to failure under stress to gain more than face value, it is necessary to demonstrate equivalent performance levels between those who learn implicitly and those who learn explicitly.

Concurrent secondary tasks affect various areas of working memory. Working memory (Baddeley and Hitch, 1974; Baddeley, 1986) has been shown to drive cognitive functions such as learning, reasoning and comprehending and can be assumed to be involved in the accretion of rules and knowledge during motor learning. The main tool available to working memory is a limited-capacity central executive which controls attention and co-ordinates a number of subsidiary slave systems; one of which – the phonological loop – plays a role in dealing with speech-based information (verbal knowledge).

Random-letter generation is generally expected to place demands on the central executive component of working memory, thus taking attention from the primary task and leading to poorer performance. Tasks affecting the articulatory loop, on the other hand, tend to consume fewer processing resources than central-executive tasks. If all that is required to prevent rule accumulation is a load on the phonological loop, then it may be possible to achieve the goal of an effective secondary-task paradigm – where performance of an implicit-learning group (i.e. with a secondary task) is equivalent to that of an explicit-learning group (i.e. without a secondary task).

Experiment 1
Accordingly, the aim of this experiment was to assess the effectiveness of implicit learning of a golf-putting task brought about by secondary tasks which interfere with the central executive (backward counting, random-letter generation)

and by secondary tasks which interfere with the articulatory loop (articulatory suppression, unattended speech).

Method

40 subjects were assigned to the following groups: Phonological Loop (articulatory suppression, n=8; unattended speech, n=8); Central Executive (random letter generation, n=8; counting backwards, n=8; and Control (n=8). All subjects were required to putt a total of 400 times in eight blocks of 50 putts; a short rest was given between each block. All putts were made from a distance of 150cm at a hole 10.8cm in diameter.

The subjects in a secondary task group were required to carry out their task at all times during putting. The articulatory suppression task required subjects to say the word "weeds" about twice per second. Those in the unattended speech group were played a tape of random English words at 75dB (A). Subjects performing random letter generation were required to say a letter every 1.5 seconds for the first 200 putts and every 1s for the final 200 putts; subjects were not allowed to utter stereotyped sequences of letters e.g. ABC or BBC. Those in the counting backwards group were required to count backwards from 1200. Control group subjects did not perform a concurrent secondary task.

After completion of the 400 putts subjects were required to complete written verbal protocols divulging any "rules, knowledge or methods" they had used during putting. The protocols were later scored by two independent raters for explicit rules relating to putting.

Results

Rules. Calculation of a Pearson product-moment correlation coefficient showed that the independent raters were in agreement on the number of explicit rules written down by each subject (r=.91, p<.05). These ratings were combined and the mean number of rules accrued in each condition is shown in Figure 1.

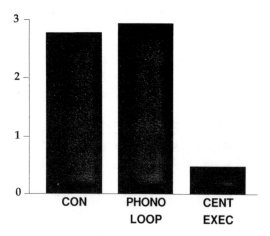

Figure 1: Mean number of rules reported by subjects in Control (CON), Phonological Loop (PHONO LOOP) and Central Executive (CENT EXEC) groups.

A one-way ANOVA showed a significant effect of secondary task (F(2,37) = 24.59, p<.05). Post-hoc tests for differences with Fisher's Least-Significant Differences procedure showed significant differences between the Central Executive group and both Phonological Loop and Control groups (p<.05). There was no significant difference between the Control and the Phonological Loop groups (p>.05).

Performance. A two-way ANOVA (Group x Block; 3 x 4) with repeated measures on the second factor showed there to be a main effect of Blocks (F(3,111) = 39.84, p<.05) indicating that learning had occurred. A significant main effect for Groups (F(2,37) = 5.46, p<.05) was also present, suggesting that the Central Executive group had a generally lower level of performance throughout the learning phase. No interaction was evident (F(6,111) = .40, p>.05).

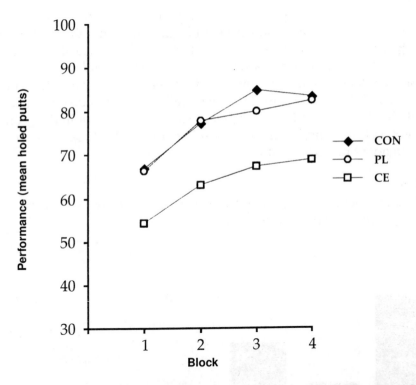

Figure 2. Mean number of putts holed as a function of Blocks for the Control (CON), Phonological Loop (PL) and Central Executive (CE) groups.

Discussion

The secondary tasks loading on the phonological loop component of working memory failed to suppress the accumulation of rules. Indeed, subjects gained as many, if not more, rules than those in the Control condition, in which no secondary task was required. Moreover, as can be seen in Figure 2, performance was not affected by disruption of the phonological loop. As shown by Masters

(1992) and Hardy et al. (1996), disruption of the central executive via random letter generation or counting backwards prevents rule accumulation, but at the expense of a detrimental effect upon performance.

Experiment 2

Despite the failure of phonological loop tasks in this case, the possibility remains that for a more demanding primary task suppression may become effective, as greater processing resources are needed to maintain performance on the primary task. Accordingly, in the following experiment a ballistic aiming task (dart-throwing) was used as a primary task. Unattended speech and counting backwards were dropped as secondary tasks, since it was felt that their effects were virtually identical to those of articulatory suppression and random-letter generation respectively.

Method

Twenty-five subjects were assigned randomly to the following groups: Control (n=9), Articulatory Suppression (n=8); and Random Letter-Generation (n=8). Secondary task methodologies were identical to those used in the previous experiment. Each subject was required to throw 100 times (in 10 blocks of 10 with a short rest period after 50 throws) at a target of four concentric circles of diameter 4.4, 22, 37.2 and 60cm. Throws were made from a distance of 200cm. When all 100 throws had been completed subjects were required to complete verbal protocols in a similar manner as in Experiment 1. These were scored by two independent raters as before.

Results

Rules. The independent raters were in close agreement (r=.93, p<.05) and so their ratings were combined (Figure 3).

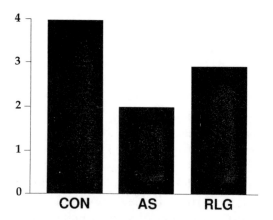

Figure 3: Mean number of rules reported by subjects in control (CON), articulatory suppression (AS) and random letter-generation (RLG) groups.

A one-way ANOVA showed a significant effect of Group (F(2,22) = 3.72, p<.05). Post-hoc tests for differences using Fisher's LSD procedure showed a significant difference between the Control and Phonological Loop groups (p<.05), but not between the Control and the Random Letter-Generation groups (p>.05).
Performance. A two-way analysis of variance (Group x Block; 3 x 10) with repeated measures on the second factor showed a significant main effect of Blocks (F(9,198) = 5.91, p<.05). Neither a main effect of Groups (F(2,22) = 1.77, p>.05) nor an interaction (F(18, 198) = 1.23, p>.05) was found.

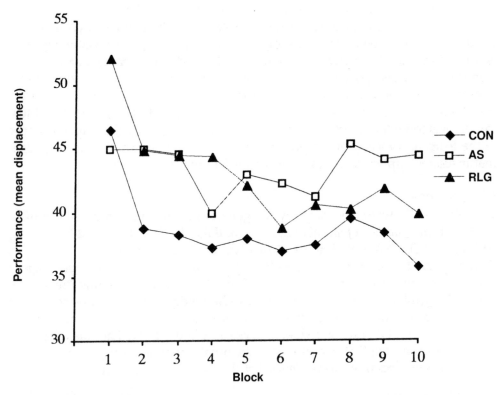

Figure 4. Mean displacement of darts from the centre of the target as a function of Blocks for the Control (CON), Articulatory Suppression (AS) and Random Letter-Generation (RLG) groups.

Discussion

In the second experiment, using the more demanding dart-throwing task, articulatory suppression was effective in preventing the accumulation of explicit rules; somewhat surprisingly, random letter-generation did not do so to a significant degree. However, there did appear to be a clear trend toward lower rules than in the Control group. This trend, in conjunction with results from previous experiments (Masters,1992; Hardy et al., 1996) suggests that a larger sample size would produce a significant difference. A concern that arises is the performance of the Articulatory Suppression group which gradually deteriorated after Block 4. It is possible that by this point dual-task fatigue, specific to the articulatory suppression task, had resulted in a need for attention from the central executive in order to continue carrying out articulatory suppression. In other words, the articulatory-secondary task had become a central-executive task.

The results of these experiments do not provide conclusive support for the view that interference with the phonological loop is sufficient to prevent explicit rule accumulation. The results of Experiment 1 demonstrate virtually identical rule formation by subjects in the Phonological Loop group to those in the Control group. Experiment 2 suggests that phonological loop secondary tasks may be effective when the primary motor task is sufficiently demanding – but the apparent fatigue effect was undoubtedly a problem.

Further work manipulating the complexity of the primary motor task or the diversity of the secondary task and possibly exploring other secondary tasks is needed in order to clarify these rather murky findings. Perhaps turning away from secondary task paradigms would be of value. Other, less demanding methods of causing implicit learning of motor skills should be sought to avoid the problems of degraded performance during learning. Indeed, until this problem can be overcome the question remains of whether it is really the implicit nature of the learning process, or simply the effect of the secondary task as a stressor that insulates implicit learners against skill failure under stress.

References

Baddeley, A.D. (1966) The capacity for generating information by randomisation. *Quarterly Journal of Experimental Psychology, 18,* 119–129.

Baddeley, A.D. (1986) *Working Memory.* Oxford: Oxford University Press.

Baddeley, A.D. and Hitch, G. (1974). In G.A. Bower (Ed.) *The Psychology of Learning and Motivation.* Vol 8, 47–89. New York: Academic Press.

Hardy, L., Mullen, R. and Jones, G. (1996) Knowledge and conscious control of motor actions under stress. *British Journal of Psychology, 87,* 621–636.

Masters, R.S.W. (1992) Knowledge, knerves and know-how: The role of implicit versus explicit knowledge in the breakdown of a complex motor skill under pressure. *British Journal of Psychology, 83,* 343–356.

6

Measuring cognitive enhancement: Cross-cultural variations and the link with psychological skills training

Craig Mahoney and Orla O'Leary

Socialist eastern European countries placed great emphasis on sporting excellence. As a consequence, sports sciences – and in particular sport psychology – received great credibility. This interest in the use of psychology in sport prompted countries such as USA, Canada, Australia and West Germany to invest in sport psychology. The American athletics team took 14 sport psychologists to the 1988 Olympic Games, while the UK took just one and Ireland did not take any. In 1992 the UK team took seven psychologists with them and Ireland took one; while in 1996 the UK took nine. While the increase in psychological support does not show a positive correlation with gold medals, this is not an indication of wasted effort since the educational value of such programmes cannot be dismissed (Vealey, 1994). The idea that psychological skills are innate and therefore untrainable has been replaced by the contemporary opinion that psychological skills training (PST) programmes are part of an educational process from which performance enhancement can be achieved (Vealey, 1988; 1994).

In recent years, recognition that PST can produce enhanced athletic performance has become popular (Greenspan and Feltz, 1989; Weinberg and Comar, 1994; Beauchamp et al., 1996). Greenspan and Feltz (1989), in reviewing 23 research papers using PST, found interventions (actions initiated by someone other than the athlete, designed to improve the athlete's competitive performance) were generally effective. According to Vealey (1994), interventions in sport psychology produce psycho-behavioural change which can enhance performance and athlete experience. Murphy (1995) claimed psychological interventions have resulted from competitive stress from which athletes have sought assistance. In a Recent review of the effectiveness of cognitive enhancement interventions in sport, Weinberg and Comar (1994) found that 85 per cent of studies demonstrated positive performance improvements. Beauchamp et al. (1996) found cognitive-behavioural approaches to the development of motivation, preparation and putting performance were effective in creating performance enhancement for novice golfers.

The often-held premise that interventions should immediately result in improved sporting performance fails to acknowledge the multitude of variables which can militate against the assimilation of new information, techniques and strategies into daily training routines. The transfer of this enhancement into competitive performance, often accounting for less than five per cent of total time associated with the sport, is not guaranteed. This is not to deny accountability and the need to produce performance improvements through intervention, but shows awareness that changes in cognitive strategies likely to produce optimum performance are slow to occur.

An understanding of the limitations in PST programmes is fundamental to their appropriate assessment. Since PST programmes are usually assessed on performance outcomes, it seems sensible to seek methods of assessment which will establish cognitive enhancement, are valid and reliable, can discern improvements and are associated with peak performance in sport. This should occur in addition to, and perhaps before, positive performance outcome is used to assess effectiveness.

Proper assessment of the effects of PST programmes is of vital importance. However, prior baseline assessment of psychological skill as part of a needs analysis is essential in determining individual athlete interventions. Strategies including interview techniques, performance profiling, observation and the administration of psychological inventories have all been used to measure psychological skills (Mahoney et al., 1987; Orlick and Partington, 1988; Butler and Hardy, 1992). In an attempt to quantify cognitive skills, Mahoney et al. (1987) established characteristics of common and elite performers, and subsequently produced the Psychological Skills Inventory in Sport (PSIS), which he altered to assess intensity (PSIS R-5; Mahoney, 1989). PSIS R-5 is designed to assess cognitive strategies to control anxiety, confidence, concentration, mental preparation, motivation and team focus. Mahoney (1989) acknowledged that this is a developmental tool, though several full papers have been published using the questionnaire (White and Croce, 1992; Chartrand et al., 1992; Cox and Liu, 1993) and numerous abstracts (Bull, 1990; Morrison et al., 1996; Mahoney et al., 1996).

The assessment of psychological skills has often been carried out using a battery of psychometric tests. However, this shotgun approach is problematic since scales measuring isolated skills tend to originate from widely different theoretical viewpoints which can increase administrative and interpretative time and error (Nelson and Hardy, 1992). While some sport-specific questionnaires have been developed, few instruments have been developed to measure a range of psychological skills associated with general sporting performance (Nelson and Hardy, 1992), though PSIS R-5 is one such measure.

PSIS R-5 is a 45-item scale with a five-point Likert response scale in which Mahoney (1989) reported an internal consistency, with a split-half correlation coefficient of 0.567 and Spearman-Brown coefficient of 0.724. Other authors (White and Croce, 1992; White, 1993) reported Cronbach alpha reliability coefficients for the six subscales ranging from $r=0.69$ to $r=0.77$ and $r=0.69$ to $r=0.84$, respectively. Bull (1990) found acceptable reliability for the anxiety management and confidence subscales and claimed that the results provided construct validity for these dimensions of the scale.

Despite these positive results, the PSIS R-5 has been criticised (Nelson and Hardy, 1992; Chartrand et al., 1992). Chartrand et al. (1992) found an internal consistency of -0.34 for the mental preparation subscale and questioned its validity. However, the possibility was raised that the analyses may have been too restrictive and continued research focusing on additional sports populations to increase sample size was strongly recommended.

Curiously, sport sciences other than psychology appear to walk on hallowed turf regarding the need to show improved performance following intervention. It seems that only laboratory-based changes are needed in physiology and mechanics for coaches, athletes and parents to be satisfied. While not wishing to suggest that psychology should be acceptable on the same basis, it seems curious that psychological interventions are evaluated largely on performance outcomes (Daw and Burton, 1994).

This study sought to investigate the effectiveness of the PSIS R-5 for measuring cognitive enhancement in a large cross-cultural study between British and Irish sports performers. No study has considered the effect of PST on psychological skills, and therefore the purpose of this study was to investigate differences in psychological skills of athletes from different levels, sports, genders, nationalities, types of sport (individual or team), intensities of training and uses of PST. Quantification of such changes is difficult and often ignored; the production of heuristic findings is valued by coaches and athletes, but has received limited empirical support (White, 1993; Mahoney et al., 1987).

Methods

Athletes (n=108) from rugby, camogie and swimming were included in this study which assessed mental strategies and self-reports before exposure to PST (Table 1). The performances of each athlete were categorized as "more successful" or "less successful", which roughly corresponded with elite (national and international) and average (club and county) respectively.

Each participant was required to complete two questionnaires. The first

Table 1. Sample characteristics: distribution of sample (n=108) and mean ages for significant factors

Sport	Rugby (26.6±5.4yrs)		Swim. (17.7±3.4yrs)		Camogie (24.3±5.2yrs)***	
	N	%	N	%	N	%
	46	43	28	26	34	31
Gender	F (21.75.8yrs)		M (25.26.0yrs)**			
	N	%	N	%		
	56	52	52	48		
Ind/Team	Ind. (17.73.4yrs)		Team (25.65.4yrs)***			
	N	%	N	%		
	28	26	80	74		
Level	More Successful		Less Successful			
	N	%	N	%		
	51	47	57	53		
Nationality	Irish		British			
	N	%	N	%		
	34	31	74	69		

** p<.001
***p<.01

was a personal data questionnaire which sought information related to the athlete's age, sex, level of participation and number of hours spent training. Questions related to their understanding and involvement in cognitive enhancement strategies for sport were also answered.

The second questionnaire, PSIS R-5, was used to assess sports related cognitive skills. The 45-item questionnaire uses a five-point Likert scale for response intensity and had been factor analysed into categories labelled anxiety management (10 items), concentration (six items), confidence (nine items), mental preparation (six items), motivation (seven items) and team emphasis (seven items).

Data were analysed using a range of statistics, ANOVA with sex, sport, nationality, training and level of participation as independent variables, with appropriate post hoc testing where necessary.

Results

The PSIS R-5 results described in Table 2 provide evidence of differences in cognitive strategies between groups based on sex, sport, nationality, team or individual, and amount of training. Previously, Mahoney et al. (1987) and Cox and Liu (1993) found sex differences in confidence, a finding supported in this study. The cross-cultural study of Cox and Liu also found differences in confidence and motivation between Chinese and American athletes. The present study found mental preparation and team emphasis to be significantly different, with British athletes using more mental preparation (imagery), and Irish athletes being more team-oriented.

From the three sports investigated, the results showed a significant difference in confidence and team emphasis. Post-hoc testing showed that rugby players were more confident than either swimmers or camogie players, while camogie players were more team-oriented than swimmers or rugby players. These findings may be influenced by the older mean age of the rugby players and their male dominance, while the team emphasis could be a result of the strong social influences, passion and bonding inherent in Irish sporting culture.

A comparison of individual athletes and team players showed that mental preparation was more commonly used by those from individual sports. Given that swimming was the only individual sport included in the study, this finding needs further investigation.

Table 2. ANOVA results of PSIS R-5 subscales

Independent Variable	F-ratio	Significance	Dependent Variable
Sex	$F_{1,107} = 9.36$	$P < 0.01$	Confidence
Sport	$F_{2,106} = 4.09$	$P < 0.05$	Confidence
	$F_{2,106} = 4.01$	$P < 0.05$	Team emphasis
Nationality	$F_{1,107} = 5.24$	$P < 0.05$	Mental preparation
	$F_{1,107} = 7.88$	$P < 0.01$	Team emphasis
Individual or team	$F_{1,107} = 4.02$	$P < 0.05$	Mental preparation
Training	$F_{3,105} = 3.07$	$P < 0.05$	Motivation

Finally, the amount of training was considered as a further independent variable. As expected, athletes who trained hard for long periods (more than seven hours per week) showed a significantly higher level of motivation than those who did less. Non-significant differences were found between performers who had self-reported previous involvement in PST programmes (or who currently used cognitive enhancement strategies as part of their training) and those who had not been exposed to PST and did not currently use any enhancement techniques. This was also true for the level of performance in which more- and less-successful athletes showed no difference in psychological skills.

Discussion

This study has shown that cognitive skills can be evaluated using questionnaires like PSIS R-5. The information has value as part of needs analysis and performance profiles, which should be integrated into the initial stages of any cognitive intervention. While conclusive evidence surrounding the assessment of change in psychological skills has not been established in this study, PSIS R-5 may still be sensitive to change using a more appropriate methodology. What is clear is that the study lacked the robustness to determine correctly the effectiveness of enhancement assessment; a recommendation is for athletes to complete pre- and post-assessment of cognitive strategies in controlled PST intervention studies.

PST programmes involve problems such as adherence (Bull, 1991). While the present study did not attempt to use an intervention model, it did seek to determine the effect of such programmes on the basis of self-reported exposure and the use of enhancement strategies. Over 75 per cent of the sample believed mental and physical preparations were equally important. However, only 32 per cent made use of some form of cognitive or behavioural enhancement strategy, due in part to a lack of experience or knowledge about where to acquire such information. However, the general consensus was positive regarding the use, acceptance and appropriateness of PST programmes in sport. This is a view supported by Vealey (1994) who emphasized the need to educate athletes about available strategies.

The study highlighted a number of important issues surrounding the measurement of cognitive enhancement and has identified the need to consider cultural variations as a significant determinant in studies of this type. PSIS R-5 is sufficiently sensitive to determine differences between groups based on sex, sport, training, nationality, and team or individual preference, though it does not distinguish between athletes who claim self-reported completion of PST and those who do not. While this latter point could be considered a deficiency in the questionnaire, it is more likely to be attributable to a lack of quality control associated with PST which the athletes undertook. Nonetheless, the PSIS R-5 questionnaire was developed in America for elite American athletes and Mahoney (1989) has stated that it is still in its developmental infancy. Given the cultural variety within Europe and the cultural differences between American and British or Irish athletes, it is reasonable to suggest that the questionnaire should be critically reviewed with a view to producing a population-specific as variation version two.

References

Beauchamp, P.H., Halliwell, W.R., Fournier, J.F. and Koestner, R. (1996) Effects of cognitive-behavioural psychological skills training on the motivation, preparation, and putting performance of novice golfers. *The Sport Psychologist, 10,* 157–170.

Bull, S.J. (1991) Personal and situational influences on adherence to mental skills training. *Journal of Sport and Exercise Psychology, 13,* 121–132.

Bull, S.J. (1990) The psychological skills inventory for sports: a preliminary investigation. *Journal of Sport Psychology Science, 8,* 82–83.

Butler, R.J. and Hardy, L. (1992) The performance profile: theory and application. *The Sport Psychologist, 6,* 253–264.

Chartrand, J.M., Jowdy, D.P., 7 Danish, S.J. (1992) The psychological skills inventory for sports: psychometric characteristics and applied implications. *Journal of Sport and Exercise Psychology, 14,* 405–413.

Cox, R.H. and Liu, Z. (1993) Psychological skills: a cross-cultural investigation. *International Journal of Sport Psychology, 24,* 326–340.

Daw, J. and Burton, D. (1994) Evaluation of a comprehensive psychological skills training program for collegiate tennis players. *The Sport Psychologist, 8,* 37–57.

Greenspan, M.J., and Feltz, D.L. (1989) Psychological interventions with athletes in competitive situations: a review. *The Sport Psychologist, 3,* 219–236.

Mahoney, C.A., MacIntyre, T. and Moran, A. (1996) Mental skills in Ireland's top sports performers. *The Irish Psychologist, 23(4),* 46.

Mahoney, M.J. (1989) Psychological predictors of elite and non-elite performance in Olympic weightlifters. *International Journal of Sport Psychology, 20,* 1–12.

Mahoney, M.J., Gabriel, T.J. and Perkins, T.S. (1987) Psychological skills and exceptional athletic performance. *The Sport Psychologist, 1,* 181–199.

Morrison, Z.A. and Mahoney, C.A. (1996) A multisport comparison of psychological skills. *Journal of Sports Sciences, 14(1),* 41.

Murphy, S.M. (1995). Introduction to sport psychology interventions. In S.M Murphy *Sport Psychology Interventions,* 1–17. Champaign, IL: Human Kinetics.

Nelson, D. and Hardy, L. (1992) The development and validation of the Sports Psychological Skills Inventory. Unpublished document.

Orlick, T. and Partington, J. (1988). Mental links to excellence. *The Sport Psychologist, 2,* 105–130.

Vealy, R.S. (1988) Future directions in psychological skills training. *The Sport Psychologist, 2,* 318–336.

Vealy, R.S. (1994) Current status and prominent issues in sport psychology interventions. *Medicine and Science in Sport and Exercise, 26,* 495–502.

Weinberg, R.S. and Comar, W. (1994). The effectiveness of psychological interventions in competitive sport. *Sports Medicine, 18,* 406–418.

White, S.A. (1993) The relationship between psychological skills, experience, and practice commitment among collegiate male and female skiers. *The Sport Psychologist, 7,* 49–57.

White, S.A. and Croce, R.V. (1992) Nordic disabled skiers and able-bodied skiers: an exploratory analysis of the psychological skills inventory for sport (PSIS, R-5). *Clinical Kinesiology, 45,* 7–9.

7

Performance enhancement and deterioration, following outcome imagery: Testing a demand-characteristics explanation

David F. Shaw and Richard Goodfellow

While there is a vast literature on imagery in sport, the bulk of it has focused on mental practice (Weinberg, 1981; Feltz and Landers, 1983; Feltz, Landers and Becker, 1988; Grouios, 1992). There have been relatively few studies, of value to the performer, of outcome-depiction imagery. The term *outcome-depiction imagery* is used here to describe imagery of what happens immediately after an action is completed and not of the action itself. For example, it might be the mental depiction of a golf ball rolling from the golfer to the hole after being struck.

There is some confusion in the imagery literature over terminology. Mental rehearsal and outcome-depiction imagery have often been treated as one and the same (see, for example, Perry and Morris, 1995; Murphy and Jowdy, 1992; Vealey and Walter, 1993). The two concepts differ and the most obvious difference between them is that in mental rehearsal the imagery involves the activity itself, while in outcome depiction the imagery is of the result of the activity.

Mental rehearsal and outcome depiction imagery involve quite different processes, even though in practice it may be difficult to separate them. The distinction between them is at its clearest for activities in which a performance and its outcome are separate events. In golf, for example, the act of hitting the ball is separated in time and space from the outcome, e.g. the ball dropping into the hole. The distinction is less clear in an activity like high jumping, where the act of jumping is at one point simultaneous with the outcome of clearing the bar. In such activities it is hard to delineate outcome depiction imagery from mental rehearsal of the performance. Nevertheless, they are different processes, and as such will probably require different theories for their explanation. It is hard to see how the psychoneuromuscular theory of mental rehearsal can explain outcome depiction imagery effects in a sport like golf, because in golf outcome depiction imagery does not include an attenuated signal of the actual performance, but is of events subsequent to it.

So much for the concept of outcome depiction imagery. What is the evidence for its association with performance?

There are anecdotal reasons to believe that outcome depiction imagery may influence performance. For example, Jack Nicklaus referred to the importance of positive mental imagery, in what he termed "going to the movies" before each golf shot. Equally, the detrimental effects of negative thoughts are often testified to by coaches and athletes (Murphy and Jowdy, 1992).

In terms of empirical evidence, however, there appear to be only six published studies that directly address the effect of outcome depiction imagery on performance. Three of these have looked at tasks which involved gross motor skill. Gould et al. (1980) found that positive outcome depiction led to improvements in a leg-kick task of strength, explosive power and endurance. Similarly, Weinberg et al. (1985) found that positive outcome depiction led to improvement in sit-up, pull-up, push-up and broad-jump performance. In contrast, Wilkes and Summers (1984), found no improvement in a slow, leg-kick task, which measured strength. Thus, of the research on tasks involving strength or endurance, two of the three studies found effects from positive-outcome depiction.

For tasks requiring accuracy or precise motor skill, there have been only three studies. The first was conducted by Powell (1973), and was reported briefly in a one-page paper with little detailed information. Powell found that the use of a positive image of a dart landing close to the centre of the target prior to performance was beneficial to subsequent dart-throwing performance.

Somewhat more methodologically-sound studies were conducted. Woolfolk et al. (1985b) investigated the efficacy of positive- and negative-outcome depiction on golf-putting performance. They found that positive-outcome depiction resulted in improved performance, while negative-outcome depiction resulted in poorer performance. In the second of their studies, again on putting, Woolfolk et al. (1985a) found that while negative-outcome depiction led to poorer performance, there was no corresponding rise in performance in the positive-outcome depiction condition. Thus, of the two studies of outcome-depiction imagery, involving an accuracy task, both find negative-outcome depiction reduced performance; they differed, however, on the effect of positive-outcome depiction. Taken together, there appears to be evidence that positive-outcome depiction imagery enhances performance, and that negative-outcome depiction imagery reduces it.

The pattern of results from Woolfolk et al.'s (1985a) putting study provided the impetus for this study. Any time a manipulation fails to produce an improvement in the positive condition, yet produces a decrement in the negative condition, it is reasonable to consider the possibility of demand characteristics as an explanation (Orne, 1962). The term "demand characteristics" was coined by Martin Orne to describe the situation that subjects find themselves in when taking part in psychological experiments. Orne argued that the demands of an experiment will overcome the natural behaviour of participants who will operate to help the experimenter by being "good subjects" and by giving the experimenter the results which they think are required.

In the context of Woolfolk et al.'s (1985a) findings, perhaps experimental participants pick up the purpose of the study and realise that to behave appropriately, i.e. "like good subjects", they must improve performance in the positive-outcome condition and perform less well in the negative-outcome condition. Of course, in a task that requires fine-motor skill, such as putting, it takes more than desire to improve performance. In contrast, a desire to reduce performance is much more readily attainable for participants. This idea is reflected in the old adage of psychological testing that we should "believe a good result but have doubts about a bad one". Thus, it is argued that Woolfolk et al.'s results lend themselves quite well to a demand-characteristics interpretation.

One way of investigating the possibility that demand-characteristics explain the findings is to remove the desire of participants to be "good subjects", by giving them a better reason to perform well. If participants can be made to value a reward more than they value being a good participant then they should perform as well as possible, even in the negative condition.

Thus, if demand-characteristics do not play a part, the normal pattern of better performance after positive-outcome depiction and poorer performance after negative-outcome depiction should be evident. However, if demand characteristics explain previous findings, results should show no performance decrement after negative-outcome depiction imagery and no improvement after positive-outcome depiction imagery.

In summary, the purpose of the experiment was to investigate the effect of outcome-depiction imagery on performance in a way which might allow the rejection of a demand characteristics explanation, i.e., when an incentive to, "do well", rather than to be "good subjects" is provided. Thus, on the basis of previous findings, it was predicted that positive-outcome depiction imagery would lead to performance enhancement, and that negative-outcome depiction imagery would lead to performance impairment, despite the presence of an incentive to do well.

Method

Participants
Participants were opportunity sampled from a population of students at the University of Central Lancashire. There were 40 females and 40 males, ranging in age from 19–23 years; all were novices golfers.

Design
A 2 (Trial) X 4 (Imagery condition) X 2 (Sex) factorial design was used. Trial was a within-groups factor, and imagery condition and sex were between-groups factors.

Apparatus
The task was carried out on a smooth, even carpet, using a standard putter and golf balls. A standard practice hole with sprung hinges was used as the target. Three concentric circles were drawn round the hole, at a radius of 30, 60, and 90cm., respectively. The scoring system allocated four points for putting the ball into the hole, three points for a ball which came to rest in the inner circle, then two and one points, respectively. Balls coming to rest anywhere outside a 90 cm. radius from the hole scored zero.

Procedure

Participants were briefly shown the basics of putting and were given a demonstration. They were informed of the scoring system and then asked to take five practice putts from a standard distance of 6ft to familiarize themselves with the run of the carpet, the putting action and the situation generally.

Next, participants took 10 putts from a distance of 6ft. Total scores from these putts determined the distance from which participants would putt for the rest of the experiment. This was done to reduce floor and ceiling effects.

Thus a participant scoring a total of:

32	points or more, putted from	9ft
24–32	points putted from	8ft
20–24	points putted from	6ft
8–20	points putted from	5ft
0–7	points was excluded from the study.	

Once their putting distance had been determined, participants were told about the incentives.

The statement of incentives was as follows:

"You will be participating in four more sets of 10 putts, with a one minute break between each set. Your average score from these four sets will be calculated, this average will be the number of lottery tickets earned toward a certain prize. Three numbers will be picked at random after the results for all participants have been collected. The holder of the first number picked will win £20, the holder of the second will win £10 and the third will win £5. If you own all the numbers you could win the full £35."

For example, if the first participant earned an average score of 24, he or she would be given tickets 1-24. If the second participant earned an average score of 28 then he or she will be given tickets 24-52 and so on.

Following the explanation of incentives, participants were asked to take 10 putts from their assigned distance. Next, they were asked questions about their sporting life, in order to fill in a minute between the first and second set of putts. Participant then took a further 10 putts. The total score from both sets of putts made up the pre-test score.

It was at this point that participants were assigned to one of four conditions. In the three imagery conditions participants were given a standard image to imagine. They were asked to image at normal speed and from an internal perspective. They were asked to practice the image twice and a check was made to ensure that they were able to see the image clearly. Participants who could not clearly see the image continued with the experiment, but their scores were not included in the analysis; three people were excluded in this way.

The four conditions were as follows:

Performance mental rehearsal plus positive-outcome depiction

Participants in this group were told to imagine themselves standing over the ball with the putter in their hands and making a "gentle but firm stroke", and to imagine the ball "rolling, rolling right into the hole".

Performance mental rehearsal plus negative-outcome depiction
Participants in this group were given the same imagery instructions as the first group, except that they were told to imagine the ball "rolling, rolling towards the cup, but at the last second missing narrowly".

Performance mental rehearsal only
Participants in this group were given only the first part of the imagery instructions which related to mental rehearsal, and not the outcome depiction imagery. Thus, this group imagined standing over the ball, with the putter in their hand, and making a gentle putting stroke. At this point they were asked to open their eyes and not to imagine the outcome of their stroke.

Control group
Participants in this group waited for approximately one minute between pre and post-test, and were also asked to wait for one minute, between the first and second set of 10 putts in the post-test. This was in place of the mental rehearsal procedure engaged in by the other groups.

The post-test also consisted of two sets of 10 putts. Participants in the imagery conditions were asked to rehearse their image for a period of one minute between their first and second block of putts. Following the post-test, participants were asked whether they had been able to see their image clearly throughout the post-test. Again, the scores of participants who imaged incorrectly were not used in the results. The scores for each set of putts were added to give the aggregate post-test score.

Results

Table 1: Means and standard deviations, for male and female putting performance scores, from pre- to post-manipulation.

| | Pre-test | | | | Post-test | | | |
| | Male | | Female | | Male | | Female | |
	M	SD	M	SD	M	SD	M	SD
Positive outcome description plus mental rehearsal	48.0	6.52	41.5	5.32	60.4	5.13	53.8	8.77
Negative outcome description plus mental rehearsal	54.3	6.18	41.3	10.9	47.9	8.6	37.2	9.5
Control	48.1	3.7	40.6	7.67	51.1	4.18	47.2	7.67
Mental rehearsal only	52.3	5.54	45.5	6.35	55.2	4.42	51.3	4.19

A 2x4x2 ANOVA showed that there was a significant main effect for trial $F(1,72)=55.57$, $p<.001$, with participants scoring higher at post-test than pre-test. There was a significant main effect for sex $F(1,72)=26.42$, $p<.001$ with men scoring higher than women. There was a significant main effect for condition $F(3,72)=4.33$, $p<.01$.

There were two significant two way interactions: a trial by sex interaction $F(1,72)=3.98$, $p=.05$, indicated that female participants improved more from trial one to trial two. Finally, there was a significant trial by condition interaction $F(3,72)=43.78$, $p<.001$.

Post Hoc Tukey tests revealed significant differences for all four conditions from pre- to post-test at $p<0.01$.

Discussion

The results suggest that the use of outcome-depiction imagery influenced subsequent performance. Specifically, it was found that positive-outcome depiction imagery produced performance enhancement, and that negative outcome depiction imagery produced performance decrement.

The control group also showed an improvement from pre- to post-manipulation, and it is quite probable that this was due to practice effects. A future study might usefully increase the amount of practice given before testing. Another solution, would be to use skilled golfers. This would widen the knowledge base in this area, since previous studies have focused on novice performers.

There was an improvement in performance, from pre- to post-manipulation in the mental rehearsal only group. However, the magnitude of the increase was much smaller than for the positive outcome depiction condition and was similar to the size of the increase in the control group, suggesting that it too, may have been caused by practice effects. Indeed, it is surprising to find rehearsal effects, given the brief rehearsal period available to participants.

The pattern of these results mirrors those of Woolfolk et al. (1985). In relation to the demand-characteristics issue, despite the incentive to do well, scores fell significantly in the negative outcome depiction imagery condition. This suggests that demand characteristics do not explain Woolfolk et al.'s findings, namely that there was a drop in performance in the negative condition with no accompanying rise in the positive one.

It is possible that the incentive offered to participants was not sufficient to overcome demand characteristics inherent in the experimental situation. However, the financial incentive was relatively valuable to the participants – all students – and informal discussion revealed that many participants appeared motivated by it. Participants also knew that the odds of winning were better than in many lottery draws; it being restricted solely to the experimental participants. The finding that there was a significant increase in performance in the positive-outcome imagery condition, also argues against the demand-characteristics explanation, since it is difficult to improve in a task requiring fine-motor skills just because you want to be a "good subject".

On the basis of this study there is little evidence that previous findings on outcome depiction imagery are an artefact of the experimental situation; rather, the results suggest a real effect which should be investigated further in order to examine its robustness and the extent to which it can be found in highly-skilled performers.

References

Feltz, D.L. and Landers, D.M. (1983) The effects of mental practice on motor skill learning and performance: a meta-analysis. *Journal of Sport Psychology, 5,* 25–57.

Feltz, D.L., Landers, D.M. and Becker, B.J. (1988) A revised meta-analysis of the mental practice literature on motor skill learning. In D. Druckman and J. Swets (Eds), *Enhancing Human Performance: Issues, Theories and Techniques.* (pp. 1–65). Washington DC: National Academy Press.

Gould, D., Weinberg, R.S. and Jackson, A. (1980) Mental preparation strategies, cognitions and strength performance. *Journal of Sport Psychology, 2,* 329–339.

Grouios, G. (1992). Mental practice: a review. *Journal of Sport Behavior, 15,* 42–59.

Murphy, S.M. and Jowdy, D.P. (1992) Imagery and mental practice. In T.S. Horn (Ed.), Advances in Sport Psychology. (pp. 221–250). Champaign, IL: Human Kinetics Publishers.

Orne, M.T. (1962) On the social psychology of the psychological experiment: demand characteristics and their implications. *American Psychologist, 17,* 776–783.

Perry, C. and Morris, T. (1995) Mental Imagery in Sport. In T. Morris and J. Summers (Eds), *Sport Psychology: Theory Applications and Issues.* (pp. 339–385). New York: John Wiley.

Powell, G.E. (1973) Negative and positive mental practice in motor skill acquisition. *Perceptual and Motor Skills, 312*

Vealey, R.S. and Walter, S.M. (1993) Imagery training for performance enhancement and personal development. In J.M. Williams (Ed.), *Applied Sport Psychology: Personal Growth to Peak Performance.* London: Mayfield.

Weinberg, R.S. (1981) The relationship between mental preparation strategies and motor performance: a review and critique. *Quest, 33,* 195–213.

Weinberg, R., Jackson, A. and Seabourne, T. (1985) The effects of specific vs. non-specific mental preparation strategies on strength and endurance performance. *Journal of Sport Behavior, 8,* 175–180.

Wilkes, R.L. and Summers, J.J. (1984) Cognitions, mediating variables and strength performance. *Journal of Sport Psychology, 6,* 351–359.

Woolfolk, R.L., Murphy, S.M., Gottesfeld, D. and Aitken, D. (1985a) Effects of mental rehearsal of task motor activity and mental depiction of task outcome on motor skill performance. *Journal of Sport Psychology, 7,* 191–197.

Woolfolk, R.L., Parrish, W. and Murphy, S.M. (1985b). The effects of positive and negative imagery on motor skill performance. *Cognitive Therapy and Research, 9,* 335–341.

8

The importance of measuring athletes' emotional states during sports performance

Marc Jones, Roger Mace and Claire Stockbridge

The aim of this paper is to discuss briefly the limitations of relying on pre-performance measures of athletes' emotional states. It is suggested that pre-performance measures do not reliably indicate how athletes feel during sports performance. As a consequence, pre-performance measures are considered inadequate tools for assessing the effectiveness of mental skills interventions designed to improve athletes' emotional control. A recently-completed study by the authors is outlined to provide preliminary evidence in support of this view.

Limitations of pre-performance measures
The influence that an athlete's emotional state has on sports performance has long been of interest to psychologists, for example research has been carried out on the relationship between competitive anxiety and performance, for example, (e.g. Burton, 1988) and mood and performance (e.g. Morgan, 1980). However, much of the research has used pre-performance measures of emotion and related these to the subsequent performance. This is not surprising considering the methodological difficulties apparent in measuring athletes' emotional states during performance, particularly fast-moving sports such as rugby and football.

However, it cannot be assumed that an athlete's pre-performance emotional state is a valid predictor of emotional state during performance. Indeed, Jones (1991) suggested that the investigation of anxiety levels during competition should be pursued, since an athlete's emotional state during performance can be considered to have far greater influence on outcome than emotional state prior to competing.

Furthermore, for many psychologists emotion is a transient state (Mahoney, 1989) which can alter in response to many stimuli (Deci, 1980). It seems inappropriate to rely on measures of how athletes are feeling prior to competing when emotional state can alter within seconds and continue to fluctuate throughout performance. For example, an athlete's anxiety levels may alter dramatically within seconds of a competition, beginning when a mistake is made. Let us consider the example of a cricketer who is facing a fast bowler;

he is anxious because he knows the bowler is fast and aggressive. What happens to the batsman's emotional state if he hooks the fast bowler's first ball for four? It would not be unreasonable to assume that it could change in a variety of ways depending on the circumstances. It is plausible that the batsman may become more confident and less anxious as he has played a good shot. Equally, however, the fast bowler may tell the batsman "The next one will be quicker!" What happens to the batsman's emotional state then? We can speculate that the batsman may become even more anxious, or maybe determined, or even angry. These emotional changes may result in certain behaviours such as the determined batsman saying to himself "I will not get out", or the angry batsman saying "I'll show him" and trying to hit the next ball for four, regardless of where it is bowled. It is therefore important that attempts are made to assess emotions at the time most likely to influence success – that is during performance.

While Jones (1991) recommended that the investigation of anxiety levels during performance is pursued, he confessed to some uncertainty as to how this could be achieved. However, such an attempt was made in a study with softball players by Krane et al. (1994). They measured participants' anxiety levels immediately before they entered the batter's box to receive the pitch. Results showed that cognitive anxiety levels changed depending on how important the situation was to the outcome of the game. Furthermore, situational characteristics were the strongest predictors of the intra-individual cognitive and somatic anxiety levels.

A further limitation of pre-performance measures is that they do not provide an adequate way of assessing the effectiveness of mental skills interventions. Many intervention programmes are implemented to help athletes to develop emotional control; for example, Progressive Muscular Relaxation to help cope with debilitating levels of anxiety. It would be helpful if a sport psychologist could assess the emotional state of an athlete during performance, which would provide valuable information about the effectiveness of specific intervention techniques for improving emotional control at the most important time. For example, Mace and Carroll (1985) found that stress inoculation training was effective in controlling anxiety for novice abseilers. However, anxiety was only measured *prior* to abseiling and no measurement of the participants' anxiety levels was made *during* the abseil.

The development of techniques for assessing athletes' emotional states during performance is extremely difficult, but it is clearly essential for two main reasons: to increase our knowledge about the emotional state of athletes during sports performance, and to enable the effectiveness of a variety of mental skills interventions to be assessed at the most important time, which is during performance.

The study
A recently-completed study by the authors was conducted with novice climbers who were required to climb a 5.1 metre climbing wall. They were assigned randomly to either the experimental group (n=16; mean age = 21.63 years; SD=3.12), who underwent imagery training; or a control group (n=17; mean age

= 23.00 years; SD=7.31) who received a light exercise programme. Stress levels of the participants were measured prior to climbing and on two further points on the wall. The study was designed in order to achieve two major aims: to attempt to measure athletes' emotional states during sports performance, and to assess the effect of a mental skills intervention on athletes' emotional states during performance.

Participants
The participants were 33 female volunteers aged between 18 and 48 years (mean=22.33 years; SD=5.63) and were either undergraduate students (n=30), or employees (n=3) from a college of higher education.

Measure
This article reports on the results of one of the measures used during the study to assess the participants' distress levels both before and during the climb.

Perceived Stress Index
The Perceived Stress Index (Jacobs and Munz, 1968) is a checklist of 15 words or phrases that describes how someone might be feeling, ranging from "thrilled" to "extremely terrified". Each word or phrase has a numerical intensity weighting, with those phrases or words denoting more distress assigned higher weightings than those denoting less distress e.g. "thrilled" = 1.97, "extremely terrified" = 10.72. The index was chosen because it is exceptionally easy to administer and therefore suitable for use during climbing performance.

Task
The participants climbed a 5.1 metre climbing wall along a designated route which was highlighted in white chalk. They were required to tag a sling at the top of the wall to indicate that they had completed the climb. The route required the participants to climb directly upwards to a designated point, 3.65 metres from the ground (stage 1), where a copy of the Perceived Stress Index was attached to the wall. After choosing a word which best described how they were feeling, they were required to traverse to the left across the face of the wall to another designated point 4.07 metres from the ground (stage 2), and marked by the Perceived Stress Index. Again they chose a word which best described how they were feeling. From this point they were required to climb directly upwards to tag the white sling above the top of the wall before being lowered to the ground.

Procedure
All participants attended a total of four training sessions, each lasting approximately one hour. The training was identical for both groups of participants and differed only when those in the experimental group underwent imagery training and mentally rehearsed the climb. At this stage in the session, to control for attention placebo effects, the control group engaged in a light exercise programme which placed emphasis on stretching, flexibility, strength, and aerobic exercise. The testing session followed the fourth training session.

Testing Session

The order in which the participants climbed was chosen randomly and the participants were fitted with a climbing harness. They were then taken to the wall and clipped on to the climbing rope. The participants were reminded of the route they were expected to take and where they were expected to stop and asked to choose a word from the Perceived Stress Index. Participants chose a word from the Perceived Stress Index to indicate how they were feeling just prior to the climb. They then completed the climb as outlined in the *Task* section; afterwards they were thanked and debriefed as to the nature of the experiment.

Results

An alpha level of 0.05 was used for all statistical tests.

Pre-climb distress levels

Group means and standard deviations of the pre-climb distress levels are shown in Table 1. The pre-climb distress levels of both groups were compared using an independent t-test which revealed a significant difference ($t(31) = 2.03$, $p=0.05$). The participants in the experimental group reported significantly less distress prior to climbing than the participants in the control group.

Table 1. Group means and standard deviations for the pre-climb distress levels

Experimental group		Control group	
Mean	SD	Mean	SD
5.35	1.53	6.56	1.85

Distress levels during climb

The group means and standard deviations are shown in Table 2. In order to look for differences between the groups on the reported distress when they were on the wall, the data were analysed using a 2 x 2 (groups x stage on the wall) ANOVA. Results showed that there was no significant main effect for stage; $F (1, 64) = 1.1$, $p>0.05$, or for groups; $F (1, 64) = 2.22$, $p>0.05$, and there was no significant interaction between stage and group; $F (1, 64) = 0.21$, $p>0.05$.

Table 2. Group means and standard deviations for the reported distress levels during the climb

	Stage 1		Stage 2	
	Mean	SD	Mean	SD
Experimental group	5.6	1.95	6.3	2
Control group	6.5	1.82	6.8	1.69

Figure 1 shows the mean score for each group on the Perceived Stress Index at the pre-climb stage and at the two stages during the climb.

Discussion

Pre-climb distress levels

The participants in the experimental group reported significantly lower levels of distress just prior to beginning the climb. This suggests that mentally

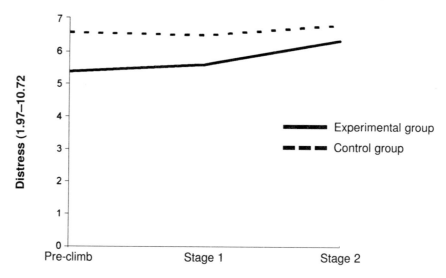

Figure 1. Group means for the Perceived Stress Index during the climb

rehearsing climbing the wall skilfully and confidently reduced the fear and apprehension that participants felt prior to climbing. Previous research (Mace and Carroll, 1985; Mace and Carroll, 1989) has shown that stress inoculation training, with imagery as an important component, can be effective in reducing self-reported distress among abseilers and gymnasts. However, there is little evidence for mental rehearsal reducing distress when used as an intervention on its own.

Distress levels during the climb
Figure 1 shows that despite the experimental group reporting less distress than the control group prior to the climb, there was minimal difference once the participants were on the wall. This indicates that the beneficial effects of mentally rehearsing the climb were reduced once participants were on the wall, possibly as a result of the high level of stress that the task caused. Another possible explanation may be that the imagery script was more relevant to the pre-climb stage, even though every effort was made to make the script equally relevant at all stages of the climb.

This result highlights the importance of measuring an athlete's emotional state during performance as it provides an insight into the effect of a mental skills intervention during performance. An athlete's emotional state is transient and it cannot be assumed that measurement of a pre-performance emotional state is a valid predictor of emotional state during performance. Reliance on pre-climb data would have suggested that mentally rehearsing the climb was effective in reducing distress. However, this was not the case when the participants were on the wall and this provides support for the findings of Krane et al., (1994) who showed that participants' emotional states are situationally dependent.

Concluding remarks

The findings from the study support the notion that ways of assessing the emotional state of athletes during performance should be developed in order to further knowledge in this area and to assess adequately the effectiveness of psychological interventions. If emotion is considered a transient state, then preperformance measures are insufficient to evaluate competitive emotional states.

References

Burton, D. (1988) Do anxious swimmers swim slower? Re-examining the elusive anxiety-performance relationship. *Journal of Sport Psychology, 10,* 45–61.

Deci, E.L. (1980) *The Psychology of Self-determination.* Lexington, MA: Heath, Lexington.

Jacobs, P.D. and Munz, D.C. (1968) An index for measuring perceived stress in a college population. *The Journal of Psychology, 70,* 9–15.

Jones, G. (1991) Recent developments and current issues in competitive state anxiety research. *The Psychologist, 4,* 152–155.

Krane, V., Joyce D. and Rafeld, J. (1994) Competitive anxiety, situation criticality, and softball performance. *The Sport Psychologist, 8,* 58–72.

Mace, R.D. and Carroll, D. (1985) The control of anxiety in sport: stress inoculation training prior to abseiling. *International Journal of Sport Psychology, 16,* 165–175.

Mace, R.D. and Carroll, D. (1989) The effect of stress inoculation training on self-reported stress, observer's rating of stress, heart rate and gymnastics performance. *Journal of Sports Sciences, 7,* 257–266.

Mahoney, C. (1989) Mood state and performance in sport. In J. Kramer and W. Crawford (Eds) The Psychology of Sport: Theory and Practice. Occasional Paper N. Ireland Branch of British Psychological Society (pp. 54–59).

Morgan, W.P. (1980) Test of champions: the iceberg profile. *Psychology Today,* 14(2), 92–99.

9

Exercise, mood and creativity in the older adult: A pilot study

Priscilla Simpson, Alison Dewey, Hannah Steinberg and Elizabeth A. Sykes

It is now widely accepted that a single bout of exercise will enhance positive mood (Folkins and Sime, 1981; Steinberg and Sykes, 1985; Plante and Rodin, 1990; Seraganian, 1990), but the relationship between exercise and creativity is less clear. Significantly improved cognitive performance following exercise has been reported by Ismail and El-Naggar (1981), Gondola and Tuckman (1986), Tuckman and Hinkle (1986), Gondola (1987) and Zervas and Klissouras (1991). However, Blumenthal et al. (1991), Pierce et al. (1993), Madden et al. (1989) and Lawless (1988) found no significant improvement. Previous studies used both single bouts of exercise and exercise programmes lasting several weeks or months and covered a range of age groups, with some studies concentrating on children (cf. Tuckman and Hinkle, 1986) and others on the elderly (cf. Blumenthal et al., 1991). Two longitudinal studies (Stones and Kozma, 1988; and Dustman et al., 1984) indicated that exercise may improve cognitive performance in the over 50 age group, while Blumenthal et al. (1991) conducted a comprehensive longitudinal study using an assortment of measures for mood and cognitive functioning. They found little improvement which could be attributed to exercise, although the correlation between improved fitness and reduced depression approached significance.

Where significant increases in cognitive enhancement have been reported, mood does not appear to have been measured concurrently, despite the widespread belief that cognitive performance is enhanced by exercise (Blumenthal et al., 1991). Steinberg et al. (1997) measured both mood and creativity following a single bout of aerobic exercise and a neutral "video-watching task". As expected, positive mood increased ($p<0.001$) following the exercise condition and decreased ($p<0.001$) following the video condition, whereas negative mood increased ($p<0.001$) following the video condition and decreased ($p<0.001$) following the exercise condition. However, the changes in creativity were less conclusive, with significantly improved performance only being shown on the Flexibility measure of the Torrance Test (Torrance, 1966). Interestingly, Steinberg et al. (in press) also reported that any improvements in creativity occurred independently of mood.

The following pilot study measured mood and cognitive performance concurrently, using two different types of exercise and two different measures of cognitive performance. Mood enhancement through a single bout of physical exercise is often short-lived, and therefore all test methods had to be short. It was predicted that physical exercise would lead to improvements in both mood and cognitive performance. It was also predicted that if improvements in cognitive performance were attributable to mood, there would be a correlation between the two.

Method

Design

Sixty participants took part in an independent groups design. Two different forms of exercise were used (aerobics and yoga), along with a sedentary control condition (collective Bible study); 20 participants took part in each condition.

Participants

Sixty females aged 50-80 years participated in the study. The majority of participants were either retired or housewives. The age composition of the three groups was as follows: aerobic, 50-64=11, 65-79=9, 80+=0; yoga, 50-64=13, 65-79=7, 80+=0; control, 50-64=7; 65-79=12 and 80+=1. The aerobic and yoga groups were recruited from an "over 50s" exercise class and from a local sports park and the control group was recruited from a local Christian church. The aerobic and yoga groups had been attending classes regularly for at least a year, while the control group had not participated in any regular form of exercise for a similar amount of time.

Activities

The aerobic activity was led by a qualified instructor and lasted for an hour. The first 10 minutes involved gentle warm-up exercises, followed by 40 minutes of marching, jumping, knee lifts, walking and jogging. In the last 10 minutes participants performed a variety of winding-down exercises while sitting or lying. The yoga activity also was led by a qualified instructor. Again, the activity lasted for an hour. The first 55 minutes consisted of stretching postural and breathing exercises that involved the whole body and for the last five minutes the participants lay still on their backs with their eyes shut. The Bible study activity was not lead. Participants took part in a collective hour-long session of reading and prayer.

Mood questionnaire

The PANAS questionnaire was presented under the heading "Statements of Feelings and Emotions", and contained 10 positive and 10 negative adjectives (see Table 1). Participants were requested to rate how they felt on a scale of 1 to 5, 1 being very slightly and 5 being extremely.

Cognitive tests

The first cognitive test consisted of nine pages of Raven's Progressive Matrices (Raven, 1958) which were part of Raven's Standard Progressive Matrices,

Advanced Progressive Matrices-Set I, and Set II. A large pattern was presented on each page with one unit missing; six possible units were presented from which the one that completed the pattern had to be chosen. The patterns became progressively harder. There was no time limit, but participants were instructed to complete the tasks as quickly as possible.

The second test was a Digit Symbol Substitution Test, which is a section of the Wechsler Adult Intelligence Scale – Revised (Wechsler, 1981). Participants were shown numbers 1–9 with a different symbol under each number. Using this as a key, the task was for participants to write the corresponding symbol in each box under the rows presented to them. There were 90 seconds to complete the task.

Procedure

Each participant completed one mood questionnaire (PANAS) and two versions of cognitive tests (Digit Symbol Substitution Test and Raven's Progressive Matrices) pre- and post-activity. To avoid practice effects two different versions of the cognitive tests were used (Set A and Set B). Participants were divided randomly so that half the participants completed Set A pre-activity and Section B post-activity and vice versa. The same PANAS questionnaire was used pre- and post-activity.

Results

Table 1. Mean differences in positive and negative mood and in performance on the Raven's Matrices and DSST pre- and post-task.

	Positive Mood	Negative Mood	Raven's Matrices	DSST
Aerobics (n=20)	-0.15	-0.7	0.35	1.40
Yoga (n=20)	0.75	0.00	0.40	3.45
Bible Study (n=20)	-0.25	1.30	0.10	-0.10

A one-way independent ANOVA was used to examine the pre- and post-test scores between each of the three conditions; no significant differences were found between scores. T-tests used to examine differences between group means showed that the exercise group's scores were slightly higher on the cognitive measures (Raven's Matrices and Digit Symbol) compared with those of the control group, with the aerobic group scores being higher than those of the yoga group. The aerobic group showed a slight decrease in negative mood following exercise ($p < 0.1$) and the yoga group showed a slight increase in scores for the DSST ($p < 0.1$). None of the other differences was significant.

Pearson's product moment correlation co-efficients were used to examine the relationship between mood scores and cognitive performance, but no significant relationships were found. However, a positive relationship was found between negative mood pre-activity and age in the aerobic condition $r(18) = 0.468$, $p < 0.05$, i.e. the older participants appeared to be less negative.

Discussion

The results of this study did not support the experimental hypotheses. No significant improvements were found in either mood or cognitive performance following exercise. The evidence for cognitive enhancement following exercise is somewhat equivocal; this result is unsurprising and tends to support Blumenthal's (1991) findings. However, while mood enhancement after a single bout of exercise is now accepted as a fairly robust finding, this investigation did not show this – three possible reasons are suggested: First, the participants were all over the age of 50 years and it may be that mood is less susceptible to change in the "mature adult". Secondly, participants were selected on the basis that they had regularly attended either an aerobics class or a yoga class for the preceding year and it is possible that any increases in mood would have been obscured by the development of "tolerance" (cf. Dishman, 1988; Steinberg et al. 1996). The positive relationship between the baseline negative mood score and age in the aerobic condition may also have been a contributory factor. It would appear that as participants get older they are less sensitive to negative mood.

Although there was no significant improvement in cognitive enhancement, there were trends towards improvement with the exercise groups obtaining higher scores than the relevant control groups. However, the yoga group showed greater improvement than the aerobic group, suggesting that intensity of exercise did not contribute to change in performance.

It may be tentatively concluded from this pilot experiment that physical exercise is capable of enhancing cognition to a limited extent. Research by Steinberg et al. (in press), where the effects of mood were partialled out, has suggested that cognitive enhancement may occur independently of mood, that is changes in mood did not predict cognitive performance. This would appear to be supported by the present data.

The results of this study remain inconclusive. Cognitive enhancement, in various forms, remains difficult to measure and an improved testing system might lead to clearer results; alternatively the type and duration of exercise may be a crucial factor, as might the previous experience of the exerciser. These results suggest that "gentle" exercise such as yoga may be more effective than vigorous exercise. The trend towards cognitive enhancement following exercise is consistent with previous findings (cf. Steinberg et al., in press; Gondola, 1987; Tuckman and Hinkle, 1986), as is the lack of a relationship between improved exercise and mood.

A more robust experimental design which takes into account other contributory factors such as music, the social nature of the activity and the exercise experience of the participants is probably needed to establish the true effects of exercise on cognitive enhancement. However, this study has tested mood and cognitive enhancement concurrently in the 50-plus age group, and would again seem to indicate that any improvement in cognitive ability is unlikely to be due to an increase in mood. However, since mood and performance following exercise have so rarely been tested concurrently, further research is needed urgently.

Acknowledgements

We thank Dr Pete Sneddon for statistical advice and the Wolfson Foundation for support.

References

Blumenthal, J.A., Emery, C.F., Madden, D.J., Schniebolk, S., Walsh-Riddle, M., George, L.K., McKee, D.C., Higginbotham, M.B., Cobb, F.R. and Colemen, R.E. (1991) Long-term effects of exercise on psychological functioning in older men and women. *Journal of Gerontology, 46(6)*, 352-362

Dishman, R.K. (Ed.) (1988) *Exercise Adherence: Its Impact on Public Health.* Champaign, Illinois: Human Kinetics

Dustman, R.E., Ruhling, R.O., Russell, E.M., Shearer, D.E., Bonekat, H.W., Shigeoka, J.W., Woods, J.S., and Bradford, D.C. (1984) Aerobic exercise training and improved neuropsychological function of older individuals. *Neurobiology of Aging, 5,* 35-42

Folkins, C.H. and Sime, W. (1981) Physical fitness training and mental health. *American Psychologist, 36,* 373-389

Gondola, J.C. (1987) The effects of a single bout of aerobic dancing on selected tests of creativity. *Journal of Social Behaviour and Personality, 2(2, Pt 1),* 275-278

Gondola, J.C. and Tuckman, B.W. (1986) Effects of a systematic program of exercise on selected measures of creativity. *Perceptual and Motor Skills, 60,* 53-54

Ismail, A.H. and El-Naggar, A.M. (1981) Effect of exercise on cognitive processing in adult men. *Journal of Human Ergology, 10,* 83-91

Lawless, W.F. (1988) Effect of arousal on mathematics scores. *Perceptual and Motor Skills, 67,* 318

Madden, D.J., Blumenthal, J.A., Allen, P.A. and Emery, C.F. (1989) Improving aerobic capacity in older adults does not necessarily lead to improved cognitive performance. *Psychology and Aging, 4(3),* 307-320

Pierce, T.W., Madden, D.J., Siegel, W.C. and Blumenthal, J.A. (1993) Effects of aerobic exercise on cognitive and psychosocial functioning in patients with mild hypertension. *Health Psychology 12(4),* 286-291

Plante, T.G. and Rodin, J. (1990) Physical fitness and enhanced psychological health. *Current Psychology: Research and Reviews, 9(1),* 3-24

Raven, J.C. (1958) *Standard Progressive Matrices.* H.K. Lewis & Co

Raven, J.C. (1958) *Advanced Progressive Matrices Set I and Set II.* H.K. Lewis and Co

Seraganian, P. (Ed.) (1990) *Exercise Psychology: The Influence of Physical Exercise on Psychological Processes.* New York: John Wiley and Sons

Stones, M.J. and Kozma, A. (1988) Physical activity, age and cognitive motor performance. In: M.L. Howe and C.J. Brainerd (Eds) *Cognitive Development in Adulthood: Progress in Cognitive Development Research.* New York: Springer

Steinberg, H. and Sykes, E.A. (1985) Introduction to symposium on endorphins and Behavioural Processes: review of literature on endorphins and exercise. *Pharmacology, Biochemistry and Behaviour, 23, 857-862*

Steinberg, H., Sykes, E.A. and LeBoutillier, N. (1996) Exercise addiction: indirect measures of endorphins? In: *Exercise Addiction: Motivation for Participation in Sport and Exercise.* British Psychological Society Occasional Publication, Sport and Exercise Section Satellite Workshop, Leicester: British Psychological Society, 6-14.

Steinberg, H., Sykes, E.A., Moss, T., Lowery, S., LeBoutillier, N., and Dewey, A. (in press) Exercise enhances creativity independently of mood

Torrance, P.E. (1966) *Torrance Tests of Creative Thinking.* New Jersey: Personnel Press Inc.

Tuckman, B.W. and Hinkle, J.S. (1986) An experimental study of the physical and psychological effects of aerobic exercise on school children. *Health Psychology, 5(3),* 197-207

Wechsler, D. (1981) *Wechsler Adult Intelligence Scale – Revised Manual.* New York: Harcourt Brace

Zervas, Y., Danis, A. and Klissouras, V. (1991) Influence of physical exertion on mental performance with reference to training. *Perceptual and Motor Skills 72(3 Pt.2)* 1215-1221

10

The effect of sport-specific imagery scripts on imagery ability and sports performance

Timothy Jones

As imagery studies begin to move from the more traditional research of motor skill acquisition*, the use of imagery instruction has also increased as part of research methodology. Indeed, studies are now criticised if they fail to control fundamental steps in imagery research, i.e. detailing their imagery manipulation (through scripts etc.), checking that the subjects have imaged what they were instructed to do, failing to identify a baseline measure of individual differences in imagery ability, and measuring the subjective experiences of individuals (Hall, 1985; 1990; Smith, 1987; Bryan, 1987; Murphy, 1990). Failing to control imagery procedures have weakened the generalizability and contribution of many studies to explain the components responsible for imagery-performance links (Woolfolk et al., 1985). Although stated more than 14 years ago, it is evident that there remains a need to control imagery systematically, organize practice sessions better, and define what is actually rehearsed (Silva, 1982).

However, many dimensions that facilitate the imagery-performance link have been identified**, and these were implemented during this study. The main attempt of this study was to facilitate effectively the imagery experience of practising athletes using sport-specific imagery instruction. An imagery script was prepared, and used during a four-week imagery intervention with male judokas (participants in judo). Judo is primarily a kinaesthetic movement sport, which trains a highly structured set of closed skills, enabling an athlete to "react" primarily to kinaesthetic cues during competition. As an athlete develops their skill, these movements become increasingly complex and the symbolic rehearsal and control afforded by regular mental rehearsal was thought to be beneficial.

---

* *Studies have explored the role of imagery rehearsal in the enhancement of performance – for example coping strategies (Mahoney, 1979), muscular endurance (Feltz and Riessinger, 1990), pain tolerance (Bandura et al, 1987; Horan and Dellinger, 1974), preparatory arousal, or "psyching up" strategies (Gould et al., 1980; Wilkes and Summers, 1984; Budney et al., 1994), and skill maintenance and performance planning (Hall and Martin, 1995).*

** *The dimensions of imagery which are already believed to facilitate imagery performance transfer are vivid and controlled images (Heil, 1984), an internal perspective rather than an external one (Mahoney and Avener, 1977), relaxation (Suedfield and Bruno, 1990), short, spaced imagery sessions that run in conjunction with actual training (Suinn, 1983), and positive imagery instruction (Woolfolk et al., 1985).*

Background research in imagery instructions

Many studies have instructed the athlete simply to imagine themselves performing the skill. Consequently, many researchers who have recorded what subjects have actually imaged have reported different imagery experiences for individual subjects. After finding that athletes who spontaneously visualized a positive outcome of their imagery experience improved in performance (Clark, 1960), some researchers have manipulated the outcome of imagined performance (Powell, 1973; Gravel et al., 1980; Schlesser et al., 1980; Woolfolk, et al., 1985), and concluded that just imaging motor performance was not as effective as imagining the outcome of the performance. If the imagery experience is interpreted as negative then it can have a negative effect on actual performance and if it is interpreted as positive, it can have a positive effect. Therefore a practitioner might be interested to learn how to ensure that their athletes are having a positive imagery experience.

These results would not surprise those interested in the effects of self-efficacy, confidence or mood on performance, as sport involves all the senses, including a strong emotional component that makes up the experience for the individual involved. Any emotional "response" during imaging can be a vital component of the imagery experience (Murphy, 1990; Smith, 1987), and many researchers have concluded that the mood attached to imagery experience (particularly a positive mood) is not only more important than the content of the experience, but one of the main active components of imagery effectiveness (Kavanagh, 1897; Murphy et al., 1989; Lee, 1990).

Researchers have also learned that by using "response propositions" (key words in scripts or instructions) during imagery, they can influence what the subject actually images (Carroll, 1982; Gregory et al., 1982; Lang et al., 1980). According to Lang et al. (1980) an emotional image contains both stimulus and response propositions; the former describe the content of the imaged scenario, whilst the latter describe the assertions about the physical responses (verbal, somatic and visceral). Their research concluded that imagery instructions containing response propositions are likely to produce vivid images and elicit more physiological responses to enhance overt performance (Suinn, 1980).

In sport, elite athletes not only image more, but they use an internal kinaesthetic perspective more than non-elite athletes (Hall et al., 1990). Using an internal perspective is thought to involve more response propositions of the image (Hale, 1982). Consequently, if a researcher can embed response propositions into imagery instructions, it may significantly facilitate a vivid, controlled imagery experience. Whilst the researcher may influence the content of a subject's imagery experience (through the use of verbal propositions), the athlete can still interpret the image. This should be, and was, recorded.

A multiple-baseline, single-subject design was used with two elite male judokas over a four-week imagery intervention. Imagery ability was assessed using the Sport Imagery Questionnaire (SIQ) which assesses five dimensions of imagery ability – the audio, visual, kinaesthetic, mood, and control (Vealey, 1986) – and the revised version of the Movement Imagery Questionnaire (MIQ-R), which measures the visual and the kinaesthetic movement components of imagery (Hall, and Martin 1995).

Imagery script

Imagery instructions are arguably the most important component of an imagery-intervention programme. For this purpose, an initial questionnaire with six open-ended questions was distributed in several judo clubs. Each item on the question-naire asked about different elements of training and competitions (salient experiences, moods, kinaesthesia, auditory, visual, and tactile stimuli). Three verbal "propositions" for each perceptual component of judo were selected for use in each sub-sentence of the script (Twining, 1949).

The script consisted of a few short sentences to help the subject to relax and concentrate on the images produced. The next sentence asked the subjects to view themselves from an internal perspective (Bird and Cripe, 1986). Five short sentences – each representing a different active component of judo – were used (as described by those already experienced in the sport, i.e., visual, auditory, kinaesthetic, tactile, and emotional components). However, the auditory component only consisted of two linguistic propositions in the sentence as the pilot study did not reveal more than two auditory cues, but this did not seem to inhibit the generation of auditory responses during the imagery sessions.

Participants followed a similar procedure during training. After a warm-up, they were situated away from the training mats and instructed to be as relaxed as possible. When they felt relaxed and could concentrate on the images they generated, the imagery script was played from a tape recording, which paused briefly between each "stimulus proposition" in the script. Once the entire script had been played, they were instructed to spend a few minutes concentrating quietly on the images created. After two to three minutes they were asked to open their eyes and to write down what they imaged.

Results

The results supported the research previously outlined; not only did the participants improve in their imagery ability and their chosen skill, but they reported that the imagery script was particularly beneficial for their imagery experience. An objective measure of performance showed a marked improvement in the execution of the skills chosen by each athlete during the intervention.

Table 1. Mean percentage of improvement in imagery ability

	Subject 1		Subject 2	
Instrument	Visual	Kinaesthetic	Visual	Kinaesthetic
S.I.Q	12.5	25	25	32.8
M.I.Q.-R	45	40	32.8	24.6

Using a social-validation scale on a seven-point scale of 1 (not at all), to 7 (very much), it was found that both subjects reported being very satisfied with the imagery training and that the imagery script was easy to understand and helped to generate effective and positive images (S1 = rated 5 , S2 = rated 6). Using this same scale, both players felt that their imagery ability had improved (S1 and 2 rating = 6), and that the mental rehearsal of their chosen skill helped them to perform more accurately (S1 rating = 5; S2 rating = 6). However, S2 felt that the imagery training should have been longer. To understand this feeling it is important to note what was reported by the participants themselves during the imagery training.

Subject 1 at first found it very difficult to control the images generated and reported "flicking faces" and switching between an internal and external perspective throughout the imagery experience. However, by the third imagery session he reported seeing things clearly, being able to hear the surroundings of the image and able to control the image effectively throughout. This level of control was reported for the remainder of the intervention. However, he reported having no kinaesthetic awareness until mid-way through the intervention, which supports the SIQ imagery scores. In the post-intervention phase, Subject 1 still reported a lack of complete kinaesthetic experience during imagery, reporting "I could feel my arms, head, and feet movements, but not the whole movement".

Subject 2's actual imagery experiences were very similar to Subject 1, reporting "constantly flickering pictures" and experiencing no "feeling (referring to kinesthesia) or sounds" during the first session. The second imagery session was reported as being very similar to the first, except that if he could concentrate, he could "hear" and sense his mood in the imagery experience. However, by the third session, Subject 2 reported "hearing noises of the tournament well", "feeling the mat under my feet, the cloth in my hand, but no body movements", being able to control the picture, and being able to arouse moods during the imagery experience. Thus, by the third session, Subject 2 reported having developed auditory, visual, tactile and mood dimensions of imagery ability during his imagery sessions. However, by the final imagery session, both subjects reported an absence of kinaesthetic awareness of the whole move during mental rehearsal.

As the kinaesthetic sense is important in judo, it may be that the failure of Subject 2 to generate this imagery component effectively contributed to his belief that imagery training should have been over a longer period. Perhaps the kinaesthetic component of imagery is difficult to generate and needs more time to develop than other components. However, the failure to generate this component of imagery as effectively as the other components during the training period, had no obvious effect on the level or strength of self-efficacy for Subject 2, as both were found to improve slightly on their level of self-efficacy. Evidence from the Social Validation Questionnaire suggested that they had other cognitive mediators of performance which altered during the intervention (confidence – Subjects 1 and 2 ratings = 6; and concentration – Subject 1 rating = 5; Subject 2 rating = 6).

From the objective performance measures taken, it is evident that both subjects players improved on their execution of chosen nage-no-kata moves. It was not apparent whether improvements were valued as being significant by the judokas, although both reported feeling positive about the imagery training, but the positive effects of the imagery training on self-esteem and confidence were thought to be important to both. Incidentally, both subjects were selected for their county squad following the intervention and both won medals at the subsequent national tournament.

Evaluation of study

In conclusion, the use of imagery instructions can be manipulated effectively through the use of sport-specific imagery scripts, which contain both stimulus and response propositions related to the sport being studied. Researchers need to monitor carefully what is actually imaged before more salient and difficult dimensions of an imagery experience are identified. As the kinaesthetic component is difficult to generate, it may be that imagery studies of highly kinaesthetic sports (trampolining, swimming, martial arts) will have to programme

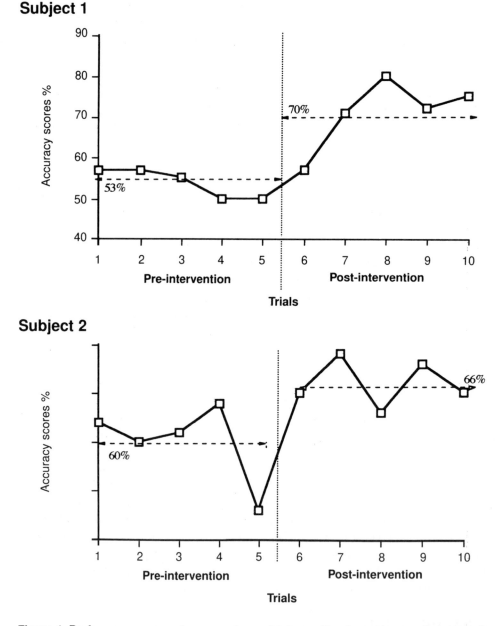

Figure 1. Performance scores from pre- to post-intervention (percentage of accuracy). The centre dashed line through five trials represents the mean performance percentage across trials during each phase of performance measurement.

more imagery sessions than those containing external cues (such as football, tennis, hockey). However, the use of effective response propositions during imagery training facilitates imagery effects on overt training.

Imagery is an ability that can be developed like any physical skill. Athletes can be trained to use imagery more effectively to aid overt training and regulate other cognitive mediators of performance. The use of appropriate propositions in the form of a sport-specific imagery script is thought to aid significantly in this development. However, more research is needed to determine not only which verbal imagery propositions are effective for specific sports, but also how to administer imagery training effectively. Each sport seems to merit its own rules with regard to these questions.

Whether imagery affects performance more because of its function in providing a motor "blueprint" of overt behaviour, or because of its effect on other cognitive mediators of performance is unclear. This paper has not considered why response propositions aid the generation of images, but this issue merits further discussion.

References

Arnold, P.J. (1990) Kinesthetic perception and sports skills: some empirical findings, philosophic comment and possible implications for the teaching of golf. In: Cochrane, A.J. (Ed.) *Science and Golf*.

Bandura, A., O'Leary, A., Taylor, C.B., Gaultier, J. and Gossard, D. (1987). In Feltz, D. and Riessinger, C.A. (1990) Effects of In Vivo emotive imagery and performance feedback on self-efficacy and muscular endurance. *Journal of Sport and Exercise Psychology, 12*, 132–143.

Bird, A.N. and Cripe, B.K. (1986) *Cognitive Processes and Sport Behaviour*. Times/Mosby. College Publishers.

Budney, Murphy and Woolfolk (1994). In Craig, H., and Martin, K., (1995) Measuring movement imagery abilities: A revision of the Movement Imagery Questionnaire (unpublished paper).

Bryan, A.J. (1987) Single-subject designs for the evaluation of sport psychology interventions. *The Sport Psychologist, 1*, 283–292.

Carroll, J.S. (1982). Cited by Gregory, W.L., Cialdini, R.B. and Carpenter, K.M. (1982). Self relevant scenarios as mediators of likelihood estimates and compliance: does imaging make it so? *Journal of Personality and Social Psychology, 43*, 88–99.

Clark, L.V. (1960) Effects of mental practice on skill development after controlled practice. *Research Quarterly, 31*, 560–569.

Kavanagh, D. (1987) Mood, persistence and success. *Australian Journal of Psychology, 39*, 307–316

Feltz, D. and Riessinger, C.A. (1990) Effects of In Vivo emotive imagery and performance feedback on self-efficacy and muscular endurance. *Journal of Sport and Exercise Psychology, 12*, 132–143.

Gould, D., Weinberg, R. and Jackson, A. (1980) Mental preparation strategies, cognitions and strength performance. *Journal of Sport Psychology, 2*, 329–339.

Gravel, R., Lemieux, G. and Ladouceur, R. (1980). In Suinn, R.M. Imagery and Sports. In: Straub, W.F. and Williams, J.M. (1984) *Cognitive Sport Psychology*.

Gregory, W.L., Cialdini, R.B. and Carpenter, K.M. (1982) Self relevant scenarios as mediators of likelihood estimates and compliance: does imaging make it so? *Journal of personality and Social Psychology. 43*, 88–99.

Hale, B.D. (1982) The effects of internal and external imagery on the muscular and ocular concomitants. *Journal of Sport Psychology, 4*, 379–387

Hall, C. (1985) In Hall, C. and Martin, K. (1995) Measuring movement imagery abilities: a revision of the movement imagery questionnaire (unpublished paper).

Hall, C. and Martin, K. (1995) Measuring movement Imagery abilities: a revision of the movement imagery questionnaire. (unpublished paper).

Hall, C., Rodgers and Barr (1990) Cited by Moran, 1992; Conceptual and Methodological Issues in the Measurement of Mental Imagery Skills in Athletes. *Journal of Sport Behaviour, 16(3)*, 156–168.

Harris, D.V. and Robinson, W.J. (1986) The effects of skill level on EMG activity during internal and external imagery. *Journal of Sport Psychology, 8*, 105–111.

Heil, J. (1984) Imagery for Sport: Theory, Research and Practice. In W.F. Straub and J.M. Williams, *Cognitive Sport Psychology*.

Horan, J.J., and Dellinger, J.K. (1974) In Vivo emotive imagery: an experimental test. *Perceptual and Motor Skills, 37*, 312.

Kavanagh, D. (1987) Mood, persistence and success. *Australian Journal of Psychology, 39*, 307–318.

Lang, P.G., Kozak, M., Miller, G.A., Levin, D.N. and McLean, A. (1980) Emotional imagery: conceptual structure and pattern of somato-visceral response. *Psychophysiology, 17*, 179–192.

Lee, C. (1990) Psyching up for a muscular endurance task: effects of image content on performance and mood state. *Journal of Sport And Exercise Psychology, 12*, 66–73.

Mahoney, M.J. (1979) In Murphy, S.M. (1990) Models of imagery in sport psychology: a review. *Journal of Mental Imagery, 14*, 153–172.

Mahoney and Avener (1977) In Weinberg, R.S. (1982) The relationship between mental preparation strategies and motor performance: a review and critique. *Quest, 33*, 195–213

Murphy, S.M. (1990) Models of imagery in sport psychology: a review. *Journal of Mental Imagery, 14*, 153–172

Murphy, S.M., Woolfolk, R.L. and Budney, A.J. (1989) The effects of emotive imagery on strength performance. *Journal of Sport and Exercise Psychology, 10*, 334–345.

Powell, G.E. (1973) Negative and positive mental practice in motor skill acquisition. *Perceptual and Motor Skills, 37*, 312.

Schleser, R., Meyers, A.W., Montgomery, T. (1980) Cited by Suinn, R.M. Imagery and Sports. In W.F. Straub and J.M. Williams (1984) *Cognitive Sports Psychology*.

Silva, J.M. (1982) In Kendall, A.E., Hrycaiko, D., Martin, G.L. and Kendall, T., (1990) The effects of imagery rehearsal, relaxation, and self-talk package on basketball game performance. *Journal of Sport and Exercise Psychology, 12*, 157–166.

Smith, D. (1987) Conditions that facilitate the development of sport imagery training. *The Sport Psychologist, 1*, 237–247.

Suedfield, P. and Bruno, T. (1990) Flotation REST and imagery in the improvement of athletic performance. *Journal of Sport and Exercise Psychology, 12*, 82–85

Suinn, R.M. (1980) Cited by Vealey, R. (1986) Imagery training for performance enhancement. In J.M. Williams (1986) *Applied Sport Psychology: Personal Growth to Peak Performance.* Mayfield.

Suinn, R.M. (1983) Cited by Heil, J, (1984) Imagery for Sport: Theory, Research and Practice. In W.F. Straub and J.M. Williams (1984) *Cognitive Sport Psychology*

Twining, W.H. (1949) In Weinberg, R.S. (1982) The relationship between mental preparation strategies and motor performance: a review and critique. *Quest, 33(2)*, 195–213.

Wilkes, R.M. and Summers J.J. (1984) Cognitions, mediating variables, and strength performance. *Journal of Sport Psychology, 6*, 351–359.

Woolfolk, R., Murphy, S., Gottesfield, D. and Aitken, D. (1985) Effects of mental rehearsal of task motor activity and mental depiction of task outcome on motor skill performance. *Journal of Sport Psychology, 7*, 191–197.

Vealey, R. (1986) Imagery training for performance enhancement. In J.M. Williams (1986) *Applied Sport Psychology: Personal Growth to Peak Performance.* Mayfield.

11

Enhancing knowledge of sport psychology within an integrated sport science programme

Derek Milne

In the 1980s there was a rapid development of psychological skills-training programmes (PSTPs), which included a range of techniques and strategies designed to teach or enhance mental skills to facilitate athletic performance (Vealey, 1988). A basic assumption of the PSTP is that athletes can learn to acquire the necessary cognitive, emotional and behavioural skills to cope with the demands of sporting competition. As a result, a wide range of interventions has been introduced with athletes, including imagery enhancement, relaxation training and pre-shot routines. In this sense, the PSTP is an educational approach.

On the assumption that the PSTP produces these educational outcomes, it becomes necessary for sport psychologists to evaluate PSTPs using multiple criterion measures of outcome. These should include performance change, but also other relevant aspects including cognitions, effort, persistence, satisfaction, enjoyment, and attitudes (Thomas and Thomas, 1994). Subsequent reviews of the PSTP literature have underlined the need to evaluate more carefully what we do if we are to be taken seriously by other professionals (Strean and Roberts, 1992). Weinberg and Comar (1994) reported a systematic review of 45 PSTP interventions, reporting that in 38 of these (85 per cent) positive performance effects had been reported, although causality could only be inferred in 20 of them. Among their suggestions for future research is a theme which is addressed within the present study, namely the need to assess a range of responses to the intervention (i.e. PSTP). They cite as an example a study by Gould et al. (1990) in which a week-long PSTP was found to change elite wrestlers' knowledge of relaxation training, visualization and other techniques. Amongst other changes, the educational programme was effective in changing athletes' knowledge about some promising psychological techniques. In a related way, Weinberg and Comar (1994) called for more extensive and detailed manipulation checks, so that we could better understand exactly which components of a PSTP effect performance change. To illustrate, McPherson and Thomas (1989) studied the relationship between knowledge and performance in tennis players. They found that the more expert players focused on higher-level concepts and had more connections between the concepts, so facilitating greater decision-making ability during the game as a result of their knowledge structure. Three aspects of knowledge identified in the literature are "declarative" (i.e. factual knowledge), "procedural" (knowing how to do something) and "strategic" (knowing tactics and how to learn). Such a knowledge structure among more skilled persons is a well-established finding from human performance research. Experts tend to have a more sophisticated knowledge structure in terms of not simply how much they know, but in organizing the content hierarchically so that different attributes of the situation are weighted appropriately (see, for example, Thomas and Thomas, 1994).

The objective of the present pilot study was to contribute to the relatively limited research on assessing the role of knowledge in performance enhancement. Specifically, a new multiple-choice questionnaire and diary are presented with which to measure the impact of PSTPs, and an illustration is provided of how PSTPs can be evaluated with these instruments. The PSTP was part of an integrated sport science "academy", provided by a nutritionist, physiotherapist, a physiologist and a psychologist to 12 juniors at a premier sport rackets club in Newcastle-upon-Tyne. This represented a little-researched collaborative approach to performance enhancement (Hardy and Jones, 1992).

Method

a. Participants:
Twelve junior squash and tennis players participated in this study, and some of their characteristics are reported in Table 1.

Table 1. Characteristics of the 12 athletes participating in the integrated sport-science programme.

N=6   Squash (4f; 2m)

N=6   Tennis (6m)

Mean age: 14.6yrs (SD 1.2)

Highest level of attainment:

National	6
Regional	2
County	4

Period competing at above level:

> 5 years	3
3–5 years	6
1–2 years	3

Prior sport science advice:

None	0
Small amount	0
Moderate amount	6
Large amount	6

As Table 1 indicates, the athletes were divided evenly between squash and tennis and had an average age of just over 14.6 years. All played at least at regional level and the majority had been playing squash for more than three years. Each had at least a moderate amount of prior sport science advice.

Other key participants in this PSTP were the four sport scientists involved in providing the programme. All were professionally qualified in their respective disciplines (i.e. physiotherapy, physiology, dietetics and psychology).

b. The programme
Table 2 summarizes the 12-week programme provided within the academy. The topics included at least two presentations from each of the four disciplines. The format was for each week's session to start with up to an hour of presentation, followed by an hour on court.

Table 2. A summary of the 12-week sport sciences programme.

Week	Topic	Sport Science
1	'Warming up'	Sport Physiotherapy
2	'Goal setting'	Sport Psychology
3	'Fitness presentation and testing'	Sport Physiology
4	'General nutrition'	Sport Nutrition
5	'Focusing'	Sport Psychology
6	'Fitness: practical'	Sport Physiology
7	'Nutrition for sport'	Sport Nutrition
8	'Warm downs and general guidance'	Sport Physiotherapy
9	'Re-focusing'	Sport Psychology
10	'Specific nutrition and integrated sport science practical'	Sport Nutrition and Sport Psychology
11	'Activation and visualization'	Sport Psychology
12	'Fitness re-assessment'	Sport Physiology

c. Measures
Although a number of measures were taken of the outcome of the programme, this paper concentrates on the two knowledge measures that were administered. The first was the *ad hoc* knowledge of sport sciences (KOSS) multiple choice questionnaire, consisting of 18 items addressing all four sport sciences contained within the programme. The four sport psychology items were derived from an earlier study (Milne and Winder, 1994) in which two multiple-choice questionnaires (MCQs) had been developed with the help of local sport psychologists. That is, the items had initially been selected from the literature (including Hardy and Fazey, 1990), placed in a 24 item pilot questionnaire and administered to six accredited sport psychologists. Only those four items that obtained complete (100 per cent) agreement between all six of these expert raters were retained within the KOSS. The remaining 14 items in the KOSS were prepared especially for this academy by the individual sport scientists and had not undergone any

comparable piloting. The four surviving sport psychology items are presented in Table 3. The KOSS was used as a measure of declarative knowledge.

Knowledge of sport sciences (KOSS)

The following questions are designed to test your knowledge in relation to the four main sport sciences. Please tick the answer you consider to be the most true or accurate. Only one answer for each question should be given.

NAME: .... **Date:** ....

1. Generally speaking, concentration, or 'focusing', is often disrupted by:
a. 'External' distracters (e.g. people, noise)
b. 'Internal' distracters (especially anxiety, worries)
c. Other 'internal' distracters (especially negative thinking)
d. All of the above

2. Pre-competition imagery (e.g. 'visualization') should:
a. Not be practised prior to competition day
b. Focus on error correction
c. Stimulate images established during practise
d. None of the above

3. As a rule:
a. Goals should be demanding, the harder the better
b. Goal difficulty is not as important as being measurable
c. To be acceptable, goals must be hard
d. Goals should be difficult, but must be acceptable

4. Goals affect sporting performance by:
a. Providing a sense of direction
b. Increasing motivation
c. Giving a focus
d. All of the above

Table 3. The four sport psychology items in the knowledge of sport sciences questionnaire (KOSS).

In addition to the KOSS, athletes also completed an *ad hoc* sporting diary, in which they self-rated (out of 10) their athletic performance, their use of sport science advice and their success in following that advice. This diary was completed throughout the Academy for all competition and practise. It was construed as an assessment of procedural and strategic knowledge.

d. Procedure
The KOSS was administered to the 12 participants during the first and last sessions in the 12-week programme, while the diary was completed regularly throughout the academy.

Results

The findings from the KOSS quiz indicated a substantial increase in the scores obtained by the 12 young racket players by the second assessment point. The scores increased from an average of 47 per cent to 70 per cent by the final assessment, an increase that is statistically significant (Wilcoxon: $P<0.05$).

The increase in knowledge of sport sciences was associated with a significant increase in the athletes' rated use of sports science advice and in their success in following that advice over time (Figure 1).

These findings indicate improvements in the athletes' declarative, procedural and strategic knowledge, and associated athletic performance enhancement.

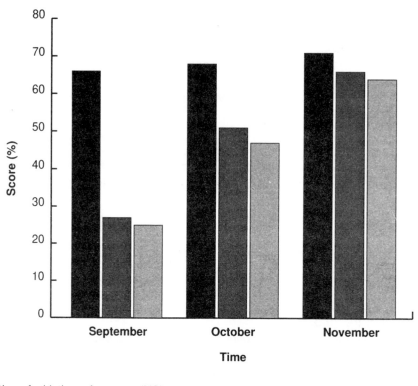

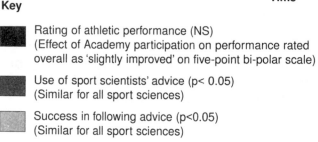

Key

Rating of athletic performance (NS)
(Effect of Academy participation on performance rated overall as 'slightly improved' on five-point bi-polar scale)

Use of sport scientists' advice ($p< 0.05$)
(Similar for all sport sciences)

Success in following advice ($p<0.05$)
(Similar for all sport sciences)

Figure 1. The Academy diary record of all training and competition during the period of the integrated sports science programme.

Discussion

The results of this pilot study suggest that an integrated sports science programme, containing four hours of teaching from a sport psychologist, resulted in a significant increase in the athletes' declarative knowledge base. The enhanced knowledge was associated with improved use of advice (procedural knowledge) and success in following that advice (strategic knowledge) as self-rated by the athletes throughout the 12-week programme. These changes were associated with improved athletic performance. The data provide a promising indication that knowledge can improve as a result of a PSTP and that this transfers to enhanced performance as one would predict from the literature reviewed above.

Two tasks for future research are now outlined. The first is the need to differentiate more systematically between the kind of knowledge base assessed by the KOSS (i.e. declarative knowledge) and knowledge about how to do something (i.e. procedural knowledge), versus learning how to apply knowledge (i.e. strategic understanding). In making out this tripartite distinction, Thomas and Thomas (1994) drew attention to the need to add to quizzes (assessing declarative knowledge) other instruments (such as interviews and experiments) to assess procedural and strategic knowledge. On a more mundane note, further psychometric work is needed before the KOSS and diary are suitable for widespread use (e.g. reliability assessments).

Linked to this methodological point is a practical observation concerning how sport psychologists can facilitate cognitive development in terms of each of these three types of knowledge. With regard to increasing declarative knowledge, the present study was based on a rather traditional lecture presentation format and therefore could be improved by using more active or discovery-based methods of learning (Milne and Noone, 1996). In order to enhance procedural knowledge, sport psychologists can encourage athletes to make much clearer links between the situation and how to respond. An example would be the traditional critical incident approach, in which for instance a video is stopped at a critical moment and the students are asked to comment on what they might do next, and what might be the knowledge base for such a decision. Lastly, sport psychologists can help athletes to develop their strategic knowledge by encouraging behavioural rehearsal of tactics and by questioning the athlete as to why a particular tactic should work in a particular context.

One convenient approach which encompasses all three types of knowledge base is cognitive therapy which relies, in part, upon the tradition of Socratic questioning. With such refinements, sport psychologists can expect to produce better impacts on athletic performance than achieved in the present study.

Conclusion

This small exploratory study outlined two new measures of knowledge as one element within the instruments used to evaluate a PSTP. It is suggested that sport psychologists should develop measures of all three forms of knowledge. Psychologists and other sport scientists should also apply action or discovery-based methods of developing knowledge within the classroom setting, and use cognitive therapy-type approaches (revolving around Socratic questioning) in their on-site consultancy. The "inner game" is a classic example of how this might be introduced successfully in the future (Gallwey, 1974).

Acknowledgments

I am indebted to the other sport scientists who contributed to KOSS and to the programme. They were Martin Andrew, Richard Hunter and Andrew Walton. The two coaches (Martin Baldridge and Alan Common) together with Sue Wilson (Project Leader) made the Academy "happen" while the 12 participants made it fun.

References

Gallwey, T. (1974) *The Inner Game of Tennis*. Pan Books: London.

Gould, D., Petlichkoff, L., Hodge, K. and Simons, J. (1990) Evaluating the effectiveness of a psychological skills educational workshop. *The Sport Psychologist, 4*, 249–260.

Hardy, L. and Fazey, J. (1990) *Goal Setting*. Leeds: National Coaching Foundation

Hardy, L. and Jones, G. (1992) *Sports Psychology: Future Directions for Performance Related Research*. London: Sports Council

McPherson, S.L. and Thomas, J.R. (1989) Relation of knowledge and performance in boys' tennis: age and expertise. *Journal of Experimental Child Psychology, 48*, 190–211.

Milne, D.L. and Winder, C. (1994) Psychological Skills Training Programme for Rowers: Programme Evaluation. Unpublished manuscript available from D.L. Milne, Psychology Department, St George's Hospital, Morpeth NE61 2NU.

Milne, D.L. and Noone, S. (1996) *Teaching and Training for Non-teachers*. Leicester: BPS Books

Strean, W.B. and Roberts, G.C. (1992) Future directions in applied sport psychology research. *The Sport Psychologist, 6*, 55–65.

Thomas, K.T. and Thomas, J.R. (1994) Developing expertise in sport: the relation of knowledge and performance. *International Journal of Sport Psychology, 25*, 295–312.

Vealey, R.S. (1988) Future directions in psychological skills training. *The Sport Psychologist, 2*, 318–336.

Weinberg, R.S. and Comar, W. (1994) The effectiveness of psychological interventions in competitive sport. *Sports Medicine, 18*, 406–418.

Summing Up

Why reinvent the wheel?

Derek Milne

I found the papers in this workshop to be exceptionally stimulating. This was because there was a diversity of research participants, topics and methods, yet a common purpose in seeking out what worked and in trying to evaluate why and how well it worked. Without exception, the contributors were well-prepared, animated and knowledgeable. The topics that were addressed got to the heart of sport psychology: what could be more pertinent than to study the relationship between how we think and how we function? The present volume provides a rich sample of variations on this fundamental theme.

However, I would like to suggest that the variation is both a problem and the solution. In doing so, I want to highlight a core issue for research and practice in sport psychology. How do we know what we know, and how do we apply such knowledge (i.e. "strategic" knowledge: Thomas and Thomas, 1994)? In learned circles, the classic form of strategic knowledge is embodied in the scientific method. With the approach we are encouraged to build on previous work, so as to create a "pyramid" of knowledge. As scholars, we should not reinvent the wheel, but rather develop existing knowledge. Yet a recurring impression from the day's presentations was that contributors believed that wheels still had to be invented. Rather than criticising the phenomenon as being in some sense "unscientific", I prefer to offer an explanation for the "problem", one that I hope is helpful.

It has been asserted that all important knowledge (i.e. procedural and strategic knowledge – Thomas and Thomas, 1994) has to be "created". That is, it is only when the learner discovers something, that this something is known properly for the first time. Kolb's (1984) marvellous synthesis of experiential learning set this out as resulting from the conflict (or dialectic) between the learners' different ways of knowing about the world. Figure 1 sets out the four basic ways of knowing.

According to the theory, the four ways of making sense of and developing our knowledge from experience are additive and at least two are necessary for accommodative learning to occur, namely one of the "action" modes (i.e. PE or CE) and one of the "reflection" modes (i.e. RO or AC). However, the truly integrated and skilled learner employs all four.

It seems to me that the experiential learning cycle helps us to understand the "problem" of re-inventing the wheel by distinguishing between personal

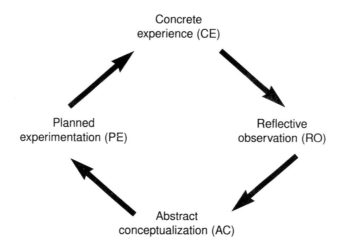

Figure 1. The cycle of learning from experience

and public knowledge, with the individual sport psychologist completing the cycle to realize something new, something that was previously not properly understood by that individual. This experience of discovering knowledge is profoundly motivating, and in this sense is valuable in spurring on researchers to the next challenging discovery. It is a personal solution, paving the way to greater public knowledge.

However, the researcher's discovery may be a problem at the level of public knowledge. Once more a wheel has been reinvented and an opportunity to build a bit more of the pyramid of shared scientific knowledge has been missed. This is one good reason not to reinvent the wheel. Therefore, my final observation is about building better pyramids in future workshops. In particular, I wish to make the case for a more integrative, cross-disciplinary approach to the development of our sport psychology knowledge. Such an approach would draw appropriately on knowledge from the other branches of applied psychology, in particular, and also on basic experimental psychology.

To illustrate this point, consider again the experiential learning cycle (Figure 1). It is an integrative model of learning and so might help us to make progress in sport psychology research and practice. For example, it may illuminate the interminable question of the relationship between anxiety and performance, as the model suggests that optimal anxiety is a necessary condition for accommodative learning. It follows that we need to move athletes round the cycle if we are to provide effective psychological skills training. We must stimulate (or regulate) anxiety if we want athletes to acquire procedural and strategic knowledge. In this sense, it is unlikely that a didactic presentation of the facts (abstract conceptualization – AC) will enhance imaginal skills, for example. Rather, the task facing the sport psychologist is to encourage athletes to test out (PE; CE) and reflect on their knowledge (RO) of imaginal skills. Only by engineering and studying these forms of learning – so as to create optimal anxiety about what is known – will we advance an individual's knowledge, as well as our collective understanding of sport psychology.

The experiential learning cycle is clearly just one example of how an integrative approach might foster research and practice. Other contenders of relevance to the workshop include greater attention to problem analysis (or "formulation") to guide the selection and application of psychological skills training in the field (clinical psychology is replete with illustrations). Similarly, conceptualization (or "modelling") of research problems might well benefit from attention to the experimental literature (e.g. human performance). Another recurring theme has been how to tackle the massive challenge of adherence to and generalization of psychological skills. Health psychology and occupational psychology, respectively, would surely repay our interest in their knowledge base in these areas. Finally, the question of appropriate measurement emerged on several occasions during the day, featuring too in the final discussion. Some presenters appeared to emphasize "mediators" of change in athletes (e.g. emotional states; working memory), a few emphasized the "moderators" of change (e.g. adherence; culture), while yet others were more concerned with change "outcomes" (e.g. performance accomplishment; knowledge gain). Such dependent variables are potentially relevant, but a coherent conceptual model is needed to show how and why they are relevant. We need to be able to answer the question "so what?" with a credible interpretation of our data. Hard data on performance enhancement are perhaps even more important. A useful cross-disciplinary resource for such issues is the psychotherapy literature, where measurement questions have been deliberated for many years. Models relevant to sport psychology are now emerging and here, as elsewhere, it may turn out that a helpful wheel has already been invented, providing us with the opportunity to progress the discipline more rapidly and efficiently than by the experiential or "reinvention" route.

References

Kolb, D.A. (1984) *Experiential Learning*. Englewood Cliffs, NJ: Prentice-Hall.
Thomas, K.T. and Thomas, J.R. (1994) Developing expertise in sport: the relation of knowledge and performance. *International Journal of Sport Psychology, 25,* 295-312